Ethics in Ancient Greece and Rome

PHILOSOPHY AND CULTURAL STUDIES REVISITED / HISTORISCH GENETISCHE STUDIEN ZUR PHILOSOPHIE UND KULTURGESCHICHTE

Edited by/herausgegeben von
Seweryn Blandzi

VOL. 5

PETER LANG

Dorota Probucka

Ethics in Ancient Greece and Rome

PETER LANG

Bibliographic Information published by the Deutsche Nationalbibliothek
The Deutsche Nationalbibliothek lists this publication in the Deutsche
Nationalbibliografie; detailed bibliographic data is available in the internet
at http://dnb.d-nb.de.

Library of Congress Cataloging-in-Publication Data
A CIP catalog record for this book has been applied for at the Library of Congress.

This publication was financially supported by
the Pedagogical University of Cracow, Poland.

Cover Design: © Olaf Gloeckler, Atelier Platen,
Friedberg

ISSN 2510-5353
ISBN 978-3-631-75772-7 (Print)
E-ISBN 978-3-631-77872-2 (E-PDF)
E-ISBN 978-3-631-77873-9 (EPUB)
E-ISBN 978-3-631-77874-6 (MOBI)
DOI 10.3726/b15112

© Peter Lang GmbH
Internationaler Verlag der Wissenschaften
Berlin 2019
All rights reserved.

Peter Lang – Berlin · Bern · Bruxelles · New York ·
Oxford · Warszawa · Wien

This publication has been peer reviewed by
Prof. Cyril Diatka and Prof. Jadwiga Mizińska.

www.peterlang.com

Contents

1 Ethics in Ancient Greece

1 Pre-Socratics

Since the central figure of ancient Greek ethics is Socrates (469–399 BC), all thinkers living and working before him are called Pre-Socratics. These include: Thales of Miletus, Pythagoras of Samos, Democritus of Abdera, Heraclitus of Ephesus, Protagoras of Abdera and Gorgias of Leontini.

1.1 Thales of Miletus

Thales of Miletus (7th/6th century BC), considered the first European philosopher, was classified as one of the so-called Seven Sages, that is according to the Greek tradition, Wise Men, who have left maxims containing general principles, norms and advice regarding the moral aspects of human life. While the Sages praised such virtues as: diligence, moderation, prudence, patience, truthfulness, faithfulness, friendship, respect for one's parents, self-control and justice, they condemned lying, avarice, impetuosity, enjoying someone else's misfortune, talkativeness, hatred and injustice. Thales has left a dozen or so wise sentences, recollected by Diogenes Laertius in his *Lives and Views of Famous Philosophers*:

1. Vouching for someone is a disaster in the making.
2. Remember your friends, both present and absent.
3. Do not embellish the external appearance, but have beautiful manners.
4. Do not get rich in a wicked way.
5. Do not let your speech raise hatred in people who share common faith.
6. Do not hesitate to favour your parents.
7. Do not take bad things after your father.
8. Whatever care you provide to your parents, the same you will receive from your children in old age.
9. It is difficult to know oneself.
10. The most pleasant thing is to achieve what one desires.
11. Laziness is a troublesome thing.
12. Immoderation is harmful.

13. Lack of manners is unbearable.
14. Learn what is best.
15. Do not be lazy, even when you are rich.
16. Keep your fortune to yourself, so as not to arouse jealousy.
17. Be moderate.
18. Do not believe everyone.
19. The one in control of oneself leads others.

1.2 Pythagoras of Samos

Pythagoras of Samos (6th century BC) was the first of Greek thinkers to be against harming animals and advocated their good treatment. In the ethical and religious community founded by Pythagoras – based on friendship, mutual help and kindness – rules for moral improvement were in force. It was related to the concept of soul migration promoted by Pythagoreans (*metempsychosis*), according to which, after the body dies, the human soul incarnates in another living being: human, animal or plant. Therefore, it is a moral duty to respect other creatures – recognizing the ban on killing animals and eating them, refusing to wear clothes made from animal skins, refraining from blood sacrifices as well as from destroying plants without clear justification. Referring to the concept of wandering souls, Pythagoreans also justified the presence of the so-called unjustified suffering, considering it to be not only punishment for worldly offenses, but also penance for the evil done in the previous incarnation. An element of the Pythagorean ethos was the daily 'examination of conscience' including reflection on one's own attitude on what good or bad was done during the day. Practising the 'examination of conscience' consisted in asking the following questions every evening: What mistakes have I made? What have I done? What duty have I neglected? Each of us should regret their bad deeds and enjoy it if they have lived the way they should. We should strive every day in this work on ourselves, because it is the way leading us to divine prowess.

In *Life of Pythagoras*, Porphyry quotes the following instructions attributed to Pythagoras: "As long as a man kills animals, people will kill one another. In fact, whoever kills and inflicts pain will not experience joy and love." "Nothing in excess." "Be silent or speak words better than silence."

"Bad language betrays a bad heart." "Whoever loses himself in suffering cannot be a free man." "You complain that you endure harm and injustice. Remember that the greatest misfortune is to inflict them." "Above all, love gods, heroes and intermediate beings between gods and heroes, but do not ask for anything in your prayers: you do not know what is good for you, because only they know it."[1]

1.3 Democritus of Abdera

Democritus of Abdera (5th/6th century BC) introduced the concept of *eudaimonia* into ethical reflection, understood as moral perfection. His works, of which several hundred fragments were preserved, were the first ethical treatises created in ancient Greece. Democritus' *eudaimonia* embraced two ideas: 'good existence' (*euestō*) and 'having a good heart' (*euthymia*). The practice of euthymia is the self-improvement of one's own personality, which should be made manifest in the heart's submission to reason. Therefore, achieving this state takes moderation in lust and action, resulting from reason. Democritus emphasized that the lack of moderation in desire is a child's characteristic, while the adult maintains moderation. Moreover, euthymia consisted of rejecting such negative emotional states as: jealousy, envious competition and hatred, and practising perseverance, temperance and self-control. Only then can a person achieve a peace of mind, i.e. the state of inner harmony and tranquillity, tantamount to happiness. This position was an anticipation of the Epicurean idea of *ataraxia*, interpreted as a spiritual balance, a lack of inner turmoil. According to historians, Democritus was the first to claim that it is better to experience harm than to cause it. Note that these words will later be repeated by Socrates, Plato and Aristotle. Democritus' instructions have been preserved in the form of maxims and moral norms: "It is better to rebuke your own mistakes than those of others." "It is better to think before than after acting." "Good is not when you do not do wrong, but when you do not want to do wrong." "It is great to think of moral obligation even under misfortune." "Bad, unreasonable, insensible and dishonest life is not only

---

1   Porphyry, *Life of Pythagoras*, trans. J. Gajda-Krynicka, Epsilon, Wroclaw 1993, pp. 11–24.

a bad life, but is a constant dying." "Three things are born of wisdom: efficient thinking, correct speaking and proper behaviour."[2]

1.4 Heraclitus of Ephesus

Much attention was given to ethical deliberations by Heraclitus of Ephesus (6th/5th century BC), who claimed that he learned everything through reflection on himself. In his opinion, the truth about good and evil should be learned through the power of one's own mind, by investigating oneself. Heraclitus spoke with disdain about people who do not ask questions as to how to act, but merely imitate others thoughtlessly. He opposed the ethics of the crowd with the ethics of the sage, where man himself seeks an answer to the question of good and moral evil, and then follows his own thought. In his essay *Letter on 'humanism'*, Martin Heidegger presented Heraclitus as the first thinker who treated *ethos* as living near to and open to God, attributing the following words to the philosopher: "Man, if he is a man at all, lives in closeness to God" (*ethos antropon daimon*).[3]

2 Sophists

Ethical issues have become an important subject of research for sophists – masters of rhetoric and eristic, who considered themselves teachers of wisdom and charged for their teachings. They did not select their entrants. Sophists promised that in exchange for money they would teach everyone how to speak, so that they would win every court case, regardless of where the blame lies. Everybody could enter the circle of disciples, provided that he could afford to pay for the education. Sophists were cognitive and ethical relativists. They did not recognize any objective values, only the diversity of opinions about moral good and evil. Ethical norms set in the form of unwritten laws and directing people's conduct were questioned and ridiculed. In their opinion, people live in a world of beliefs, and what they

---

2   G.S. Kirk, J.E. Raven, M. Schofield, *The Presocratic Philosophy*, PWN, Warsaw, p. 421.
3   M. Heidegger, *Letter on 'humanism'*, trans. J. Tischner, [in:] idem, *Build, Live, Think*, Essays, Warsaw 1977, p. 119.

believe is due to individual conviction. Morality is a set of conventions, or ways to behave that people themselves have established.

Protagoras, Gorgias and Menon are leading representatives of Sophists and advocates of ethical relativism. Protagoras of Abdera (5th century BC) is best known for his principle called the *anthrōpos metron*: "Man is the measure of all things: of things which are, that they are, and of things which are not, that they are not" (*anthrōpos metron pantōn*).[4] Therefore, there is no criterion of objective truth. Nobody can be assigned a privileged position and point of view, and all opinions are relatively right. So what opinion should you choose? – One that is more profitable or beneficial to society as a whole. Therefore, Protagoras was the progenitor of utilitarianism, proclaiming that the criterion of good and evil is what the populace considers more or less useful.

Gorgias of Leontini (5th/4th century BC) denied the possibility of any general definition of virtue understood as a moral value. In his opinion, every man, depending on their age, social position and job, has their own virtue. The virtues of a man, a woman, a child, a free man, a slave are all different. Virtues are diverse and not convertible to a common denominator. Meno of Thessaly agreed with him; his ethical relativism was described by Plato in the dialogue *Meno* and expressed in the following words: "When it comes to man's valour, it's easy to say that man's courage consists in being able to deal with the affairs of the state. And to take care of friends, do them favours and not harm them, and to be careful that you yourself are not hurt. And when speaking the valour of a woman, it is not difficult to describe: a woman should run the house well, take care of everything at home and submit herself to her husband. Whereas the valour of a child is different still, either for woman or man, another for elders, another for the free folk, and for slaves. There are other valours in existence, so it is not a problem to say what valour is. After all, depending on activity and age, each of us has some kind of valour needed in each case."[5]

---

4   Plato, *Theaetetus*, 152a 2.
5   Plato, *Menon*, 71e–72a.

3 Socrates

The central figure of ancient ethics is Socrates (c. 470–399 BC), recognized as the father of ethics and the father of European humanities. Socrates focused primarily on the philosophy of morality and human philosophy, introducing new ideas and new questions to Greek culture. He lived in Athens, held philosophical disputes in homes and public places. He left behind many outstanding followers: Plato, Antisthenes, Aristophanes, Euclid, Xenophon. Socrates' deliberations focused mainly on the reflection on man, excluding a study of nature and the cosmos. Moreover, the question about the nature of man he connected with the question of moral good, making reflection on virtue the centre of his interests. The problem, however, is that Socrates did not write; he considered dialogue, discourse to be the basis of his teaching. He left no writings, excerpts, sentences, aphorisms that we could say are certainly his. We are left with indirect transfers such as: Aristophanes' *Clouds*, Plato's *Dialogues*, Xenophon's *The Socratic Writings*. The problem is that we cannot trust any of these accounts fully. Aristophanes would mock Socrates, Plato would put his own thoughts in the mouth of Socrates – the main character of his *Dialogues* – while Xenophon, due to the lack of philosophical education, would simplify his master's teachings. It should also be emphasized that Socrates influenced the posterity not only through his views, but also through his acts that proved his faithfulness to his convictions, a testimony of being truthful. Even later Christians described him as 'a pagan saint.'[6]

3.1 Question of virtue

In Socrates' opinion, a moral person should first and foremost know what virtue is (*areté*). The philosopher was not the first to introduce this concept to the Greek language, but he was the first to give it a strictly ethical meaning. Before Socrates, virtue meant a certain capability associated with the performance of a particular social function. The word did not have ethical connotations, and it concerned the valour in life, related to a particular profession (a good shoemaker, a good cook), a social role (a good father) or

---

6   St. Justin, *Martyr*, 2004b, 10, 4–8.

a position (a good official). Polish historian of philosophy, Irena Krońska writes in her book *Socrates*: "*Areté* was first and foremost a social qualification: it was also a feature of good strategists, statesmen and politicians. With the democratization of Athenian life, the scope of applicability of this term widened in Pericles' period: *areté* may now be shown not only by a politician or a soldier, but everyone who does what he does and does it well – a good shoemaker, a good helmsman, a good cook. This democratization of *areté* as a concept was the work of the first Sophists, their ideal of efficiency in action; for them, *areté* is not only a social qualification but a praxeological concept."[7] Socrates' position means breaking away from the relativization of this concept and the search for what is common to different types of valour. In order to be virtuous, one must know virtue as such, as something universal, constituting the basis of all individual virtues. In Plato's dialogue *Meno*, Socrates utters the following words: "And so it is with different types of valour; although they are many and diverse, they all share one feature through which they are considered valuable. It would be beautiful if the one questioned would look at this and explain to the questioner what valour actually is."[8] There is, therefore, one virtue, and seemingly different virtues are only its many aspects. What then should be done to get to the truth about *areté*, understood as virtue in general, as moral valour? Trying to answer this question, Socrates was guided by the imperative of the Oracle of Delphi: 'Know yourself' (*gnōthi seauton*), and emphasizes the methodological significance of such examination. Thus, the necessary condition is to examine one's own 'I.' We should not look for moral knowledge outside, in contracts, conventions, customs, prejudices, superstitions – but in our understanding of practical sense (*frónesis*). This self-understanding is the root of wisdom and virtue. So, to get to the truth about good, one needs to activate their reasoning. Socrates equates virtue (*areté*) and knowledge (*epistémē*), which is a consequence of reason at work. To act justly means to know what is just. Therefore, if you do not know what justice is, you cannot do justice. So, what does the word 'to know' mean? First of all, Socrates distinguishes true knowledge (*epistémē*) from apparent knowledge

---

7   I. Krońska, *Socrates*, Wiedza Powszechna, Warsaw 1989, p. 76.
8   Plato, *Meno*, 70a–81d.

(*doxa*), which we find outside, in subjective human opinions and beliefs. *Epistémē* is an objective knowledge that concerns truth (*alétheia*). It can be reached only in the process of internal, rational exploration of the essence of good, or seeking a definition of the concept. In Plato's dialogue titled *Phaedo*, Socrates utters meaningful words: "So, it seemed to me that you have to resort to words and with them, consider the truth of what exists."[9] Therefore, to know what virtue is, means saying what it is, i.e. giving its definition. Thus, the search for the definition of the word *areté* will become the basic task of Socratic ethics. This search for a definition led Socrates to conclude that virtue (*areté*) is knowledge. So moral good is the same as knowing what is morally good. Let us emphasize – it is an objective, universally important knowledge, going beyond a particular subjectivism, but at the same time found in individual consciousness. If, therefore, knowing what is good and being good is the same, then this knowledge must be obligatory; it must be the source of the obligation to do good. So, knowing what justice is and being just is the same. And vice versa – one cannot be just without knowing what justice is. Also, one cannot be unjust when one has knowledge of justice. In Plato's dialogue, *Protagoras*, Socrates explains the obligatory nature of knowledge about good as follows: "The opinion generally held of knowledge is something of this sort – that it is no strong or guiding or governing thing; it is not regarded as anything of that kind, but people think that, while a man often has knowledge in him, he is not governed by it, but by something else – by passion, by pleasure, by pain, at times by love, and often by fear; their feeling about knowledge is the same they have about a slave, that it may be dragged about by any other force. Now do you agree with this view of it, or do you consider that knowledge to be something noble and able to govern man, and that whoever learns what is good and what is bad will never be swayed by anything to act otherwise than as knowledge bids, and that intelligence is a sufficient succour for mankind."[10]

9   Plato, *Phaedo*, 100a.
10 Plato, *Protagoras*, 352a–b.

3.2 Socratic method

This goal was to be achieved by a special philosophical method, based on the dialogue between Socrates and the interlocutor, a dialogue based on questions, conversation and argumentation. This conversation between the teacher and the student was not about transferring knowledge, indoctrination or moral education. Its cognitive power stemmed from the fact that the teacher helped the student to reach moral self-understanding through questions. Therefore, the purpose of this method was not to provide the truth, but to help reveal it. The dialogue consisted of two stages. The first one served to make the student realize the ostensibility of his own knowledge about good, critically look at his own ethical views and adopt a sceptical approach. This stage was called elenctics. The second method – maieutics – consisted in Socrates helping the interlocutors to reach the truth about good. The practical demonstration of the Socratic method was primarily included in the early Plato dialogues, such as: *Gorgias*, *Laches*, *Charmides*.

3.2.1 Elenctic method

The name of this method comes from Greek words: *elenchein* – to parry, return blows, show error, *elenktikos* – the one who parries. According to Socrates, care for the soul should be of primary importance to people. Elenctics were to achieve this goal by purifying the soul from residues of ostensible knowledge (*doxa*), or by exposing the ostensible nature of knowledge and bringing it to the truth. It was a negative, critical method, consisting in asking questions to bring the interlocutor to the absurd. Socrates accepted the views of the interlocutor and, starting the conversation, led him to draw conclusions contrary to their initial thesis or the widely accepted beliefs. The interlocutor would get lost in his statements, realizing the contradictions and errors in his reasoning. However, the purpose of this method was not to reach the truth about the good, but to get the speaker aware of his own ignorance. Socrates described this state as 'awareness of ignorance.' This meant taking traditional views, customs, superstitions, common beliefs about what was good and separating them, distancing oneself from them. Practising this method did not mean that Socrates had the true knowledge of good (*epistémē*). He would tower over his pupil in terms of methodology, intellectual capability and state of mind, as expressed with the words "I know that I know nothing" (*oida oudén eidōs*).[11] Speaking with the Sophist Meno, Socrates describes his attitude as follows: "For it is not from any sureness in myself that I cause others to doubt: it is from being in more doubt than anyone else that I cause doubt in others. So now, for my part, I have no idea what virtue is, whilst you, though perhaps you may have known before you came in touch with me, are now equally ignorant of it."[12]

Socrates began the practice of the elenctic method with the adoption of irony (*eironeia*), which should not be associated with mockery, derision or flout. Socratic irony is the attitude of pretend modesty, seeming ignorance and praise of one's interlocutor, which is based on seemingly trusting the competences and knowledge of the interlocutor. Socrates used it against self-righteous fools, boastful and vain people. The philosopher used to say: "empty bags are inflated by wind, mindless people – by vanity." This psychological manipulation was aimed at disarming the student from his distrustful attitude to the teacher and allow free conversation. Translator of Plato's works into Polish – Władysław Witwicki – describes the irony method in the following way: "Socrates, as he would, pretends to be incapable yet eager to learn (...). He knows perfectly well that one cannot pour from an empty cup, he is only aiming at one of the two: either to discredit his opponent in intellectual wrestling, or to extract from him an honest desire for knowledge, which begins with the admission of his own ignorance. Our philosopher uses questions to guide the discussion to his will: a series of questions and phrases, formulated quickly and unendurably, ensnares the opponent, so that he is completely dumbstruck, loses his train of thoughts and no longer knows what he had wanted. He also becomes naive enough to accept the thoughts given to him as his own, allows to be led to claims contrary to those previously accepted, reveals a complete mental impotence, and finally drops his previous position."[13]

---

11 Plato, *Defense of Socrates*, 21a–d.
12 Plato, *Meno*, 80d.
13 W. Witwicki, *Introduction to the Euthyphro dialogue*, [in:] Plato, *Dialogues*, trans. W. Witwicki, PWN, Warsaw 1984, p. 174.

Parrying arguments would begin when Socrates started showing weaknesses in his debater's reasoning. Note that this method ended with the interlocutor realizing the pretentious nature of his own knowledge of what is morally good. In his dialogue with Theaetetus, Socrates sums up this practice as follows: "you will be less harsh and gentler to your associates, for you will have the wisdom not to think you know what you do not know."[14]

3.2.2 Maieutic method

Maieutics is the second part of the Socratic method, one of a positive and constructive nature. Its name comes from the profession of midwife, performed by the mother of Socrates. In Greek, the word *maieutikos* means obstetrician. Its aim is to obtain a correct definition of the concept – the subject of discussion. The teacher's task is to guide the student to discover the truth about virtue, with the effort of his own reason. Similarly to the elenctic method, the teacher asks questions and the student answers them, but in this case the addressee is not 'a self-righteous fool,' but 'a man pregnant with wisdom.' Let us emphasize that not everyone can be pregnant with wisdom. Only one whose mind carries the grain of truth, just like a foetus in a mother's womb – which means a 'fertile and true thought.' Whereas the one who carries within himself the seed of wisdom is in need of a midwife – Socrates, who by asking the right questions, will help in the birth of the truth about good. Socrates, in conversation with Theaetetus, says: "For I am quite like these midwives; I cannot give birth to wisdom, for which many have scolded me, that I ask others, and answer nothing in any matter, because I have nothing wise to say; it is right to scold me. And the reason for this is; God tells me to receive fetuses, but he did not let me give birth myself. I myself am not very wise; never have I found anything that my soul would have born. But of those who associate with me, more than once they look very foolish, but everyone, as long as they are with me, if only God allows, a strange thing, how much they gain in their own and others' opinion. And it is clear that no one has ever learned anything from me; he himself carried his own treasure and there found a source of inspiration."[15] The maieutic method was based on induction.

14 Plato, *Theaetetus*, 210d.
15 Plato, *Theaetetus*, 210d.

Socrates began by examining specific facts related to moral life, looking for essential features and common elements in them to reach higher unity. For example, the study of specific manifestations of justice and injustice eventually enabled the definition of both concepts. In his memoirs, Xenophon describes the conversation between Socrates and Eutidemo, who wants to learn what justice and injustice is. Socrates suggests Eutidemo to put various examples of righteous acts in one column, and examples of unjust acts in another. Insightful analysis, comparing and searching for common features for a given set, leads the interlocutor to build more and more accurate definitions of both concepts.[16] Note that Socrates describes his role by comparing it to the midwife's profession. His task is to help the mind to extract correct definitions that are stuck in it like a foetus in the womb of a mother awaiting childbirth.

3.3 Voice of the daimonion

The non-intellectual element in Socratic ethics is the *daimonión* concept, which goes beyond rigorous rationalism. The word *daimonión* is a neologism, a neutral noun, constructed by the philosopher based on the word (spirit, deity). The *daimonic* experience means the interference of the divine into the life of man. The neutral gender of the word *daimonion* indicates that this divine intervention does not have a personal nature, is not an activity of a mythological deity. It is rather an intrusion of the divine element, a divine voice heard inside the human soul, which warns of an unworthy act. It is a divine warning sign. *Daimonión* does not tell us what to do, how to proceed. It is a sign of negation, forbidding certain acts in the field of moral life. Like a red traffic light or a stop sign, warning against physical danger, *daimonión* warns of the danger of a moral downfall. In Plato's dialogue *The Apology*, Socrates defines his function as follows: "It comes from the fact that, as you have often heard from me, I have a deity, a spirit of sorts (…). Since my boyish years, a voice would speak out, and whenever it appears, it always dissuades me, whatever I undertake, and never advises me."[17] The action of *daimonión* can be considered as a factor supporting

---

16 Xenophon, *Memories about Socrates*, IV, 8, 11.
17 Plato, *Defense of Socrates*, 32a.

the moral development of man, but at the same time not relieving him of the obligation to think.

4 Plato

One of Socrates' most distinguished students was Plato (427–347 BC), who founded his own school in Athens – the Academy. His real name was Aristocles, while 'Plato' was a nickname given to him by a gymnastics teacher because of his solid, broad shoulders. Plato's numerous works have been preserved: dialogues, letters and epigrams. The dialogues *Apology of Socrates* and *Critias* were written in praise of Socrates; the dialogue *Laches* concerns courage understood as virtue, *Charmides* raises the issue of reason and moderation, *Euthyphro* is about piety; *Lysis*, *Symposium* and *Phaedrus* concern beauty, love and friendship, *Lesser Hippias* – the nature of moral deeds, *Republic* – the idea of justice as the ethical basis of politics. Plato's ethics are closely related to ontology and epistemology, and so it is difficult to discuss it in isolation from these two main areas of philosophical thinking. According to Plato, there are two worlds: one of ideas and the other of things, ideal and material beings. The former one is perfect, eternal (it exists beyond time, it does not arise and does not diminish), unchanging and beyond space. The latter is a secondary one, imperfect, it exists in time, it arises (changes and dies) and is spatial. Ideas are comprehended by reason, and things by senses. Their existence does not have the same status in the ontological sense, because only ideas exist fully. Material beings only exist as a reflection, a mirror image, a shadow of the world of ideas. The true beings – ideas – are general concepts, patterns, prototypes, whereas things are their imperfect, material copies. Ideas are perfect goals defining the development of things.

4.1 The concept of the human soul

The human soul is immortal and, being immaterial, does not belong to the world of things. In the dialogue *Republic*, Plato describes a story that is to confirm his thesis about the immortality of the human soul. It is a story of a soldier named Er who, due to the wounds he suffered in battle, fell to the ground and lost consciousness. Then his soul – Era – left the body for some time and wandered around the afterlife. It saw how other souls, after the death of their bodies, were tried and received punishments and rewards. Era saw the souls of the dead who were faced with the choice of different types of life in the next incarnation.[18] The choice depended on the way they understood a morally good life. Plato combined the concept of the immortal soul with the theory of metempsychosis (wandering souls) and anamnesis (remembering true knowledge). The soul, before joining the mortal body, is in the world of ideas. There is nothing that the soul would not know before the moment of birth. However, upon incarnation, it forgets its acquired knowledge about what it has seen. Plato taught that the body is a prison of the soul, and death is its release, a release from its physical confines. However, while staying in this prison, the soul can at least partially remember what it has seen in the world of ideas. After all, Socrates' rational questions helped the slave Menon to recall and regain the forgotten knowledge that his soul possessed in the pre-natal state of omniscience (theory of anamnesis).[19] Thus, it is unnecessary to involve sensual perceptions of the material world; on the contrary, it is necessary to make effort, through self-conditioning, mental activity, for the soul to remember what it 'saw' in the world of ideas.

4.2 The idea of Good

Plato's ethics are based on his teachings about the soul, consisting of three parts: rational, volitional (passionate) and sensual (lusty). In the dialogue *Phaedrus*, the philosopher vividly depicts the structure of the soul, referring to a chariot drawn by a pair of horses. The driver is reason, while the horses are the embodiment of passion and lust. The rational part of the soul is the basis of the virtue of wisdom, the mastery of the passionate part serves to realize the virtue of valour, while the overcoming of sensuality serves the virtue of reason. The harmonious cooperation of all parts of the soul serves the virtue of justice. However, in order to live in a just and rational way, one must rise to the contemplation of the supreme idea – Good. This is the ultimate goal of our moral activity. Plato emphasizes that the supreme moral duty should be the concern for spiritual perfection, manifested in the

---

18 Plato, *Republic*, X, 614b—621d.
19 Plato, *Menon*, 81a.

pursuit of Good. Only becoming one with this supreme idea can bring the mind 'divine peace.'[20] The ratio of Good to other ideas can be metaphorically presented in the reference to the sun, which illuminates the whole world and makes it visible. Just as the sun enables seeing, the idea of Good makes what is known real. Just as the sun cannot be identified with the perceiving subject and the perceived object, the Good is not identical with knowledge and truth, but is higher than them hierarchically. In an ontological sense, the Platonic structure of the world is three-tiered. At the top there is the idea of Good – the highest metaphysical principle, the cause of all ideas, beyond all existence and all beings. From it comes light that splits into various forms, rules and values. The lowest tier is the material world, comprehensible by senses, which is explained only by what is sensuous.

If the goal of moral life is to strive for Good, then according to Plato, its implementation requires association with other people. Hence, Plato's ethics become part of the policy or the theory of life in the state (*polis*). For the various kinds of virtue correspond to three classes of citizens. The highest tier consists of philosophers – state leaders, distinguished by wisdom and rationality. That is why only they are able to manage the state properly. Bravery, in turn, is the virtue of guards, whose task is to protect the state from assault. However, the virtue of the lowest caste, conscientiously performing its labour, consisting in the production of goods, is temperance.[21] The virtue of justice differs from other virtues (wisdom, bravery and temperance) in that it is of a nationwide nature. According to Plato, justice is achieved in a state (*polis*) only when all three castes carry out their assigned virtues: philosophers rule wisely, guards defend valiantly, and artisans and peasants reasonably produce what is necessary to meet the needs of all citizens.[22]

5 Aristotle

Aristotle (348–322 BC) has included his ethical views in the following works: *Nicomachean Ethics*, *Eudemian Ethics* and *Great Ethics*. The most

---

20 Plato, *Phaedrus*, 247d–250c.
21 Plato, *Republic*, 342c.
22 Plato, *Rights*, 757c.

important of these is the *Nicomachean Ethics* consisting of 10 books, each of which concerns a different subject.

5.1 Eudaimonia

In the first book of *Nicomachean Ethics*, Aristotle asks the question: what is the ultimate goal of human life? And responds himself: the goal is to achieve the highest good or *eudaimonia*. "Every art and every investigation, and likewise every practical pursuit or undertaking, seems to aim at some good: hence it has been well said that good is that at which all things aim."[23] "If therefore among the ends at which our actions aim there be one which we desire for its own sake, and for the sake of this we desire other things, it is clear that this one ultimate end must be good, and indeed supreme good. Will not then a knowledge of this supreme good be also of great practical importance for the conduct of life?"[24] We should explore the nature of this good not based on abstract reasoning but empirically – researching what people really aspire to, what goals they set for themselves. Aristotle, therefore, accepts facts and empirical data about real life as the basis for ethical considerations. For, while observing people and their behaviour, we may say that they treat certain goals as lower, while others as higher. There is, therefore, a certain hierarchy of goals and aspirations, according to which lower values serve to realize higher-tier values. This hierarchy, however, does not go on forever; it has its culmination – the supreme goal – eudaimonia. It should be remembered that this way of thinking, typical of Aristotle's ethics, which attributes the purposeful nature to human life, action and thinking, is called teleologism (*telos* – purpose). Each of us comes into the world with some potentialities, which are activated to varying degrees during our life. The primary goal of our life would be the full realization of biological potentiality, or physical maturity, which determines the achievement of higher-tier potentials – spiritual. He who has realized all his potentiality on all levels (biological and spiritual) is one who has fulfilled his *telos*.

So what is *eudaimonia*? This ancient Greek concept means 'having a good spirit' and is commonly translated as happiness. However, it should

---

23 Aristotle, *Nicomachean Ethics*, I, 1094a.
24 *Ibidem*, I, 1094a.20.

be noted that this word has a deeper meaning, enriched with a perfection-istic thread. *Eudaimonia* is happiness and perfection put together. The ultimate goal of human efforts and the state of spiritual fulfilment. It is a contemplative life aimed at learning the truth. It is a continuous, ceaseless activity (*enérgeia*) of our intellectual powers.[25] It is the intellect at work, performed for the very work itself. *Eudaimonia* does not serve anyone or anything; it is the highest goal, closing the hierarchy of goals. A man who achieved eudaimonia – i.e. perfection and happiness at the same time – is a fulfilled man.[26] However, not all people have matured enough to grasp the highest good as a continuous rational activity. People are different and not everyone realizes their *telos*. Hence the various views about the highest good, commonly called happiness. There are those who see happiness in pleasures, in experiencing bodily delights. According to Aristotle, this is the lowest form of happy life. In his *Nicomachean Ethics*, the philosopher writes: "Uneducated people and simpletons seek it in pleasure, which is why they are satisfied with the life of usage. The uneducated common folk, therefore, reveals a very servile nature, choosing a lifestyle suitable for cattle."[27] A better form of happiness is getting satisfaction from civic activity, from working for the good of the society. For people who choose this type of life, honours are the supreme good. Aristotle believed it to be a more valuable form of life, because it increases one's rational activity. Let us refer again to the *Nicomachean Ethic*: "Men of refinement, on the other hand, and men of action think that good is honour – for this may be said to be the end of the life of politics."[28] Each of these two forms of a happy life is, unfortunately, unstable; it includes an element of randomness and dependence on external factors. For both pleasure and honours seem to depend more on those who give them to us than on ourselves. On the other hand, absolute good – rationality – does not depend on other people. It has a value in and of itself.

---

25 V.J. Bourke, *History of Ethics*, Axios Press, New York, 2008, p. 28.
26 Ch. Rowe, *Ethics of ancient Greece*, [in:] P. Singer, *A Companion to Ethics*, Basil Blackwell, New York, 1991, pp. 159–160.
27 Aristotle, *Nicomachean Ethics*, 1095b.
28 *Ibidem*, I, 1095b.21–23.

5.2 Theory of virtues

Here we have reached the Aristotelian theory of virtues, which is discussed in books III, IV and V of *Nicomachean Ethics*. For only he who fully uses reason can be virtuous. Rationality becomes a necessary condition for moral life. It should be remembered that virtue is only the result and proof of rationality, not its purpose. It is eudaimonia that is the ultimate goal of human life. Man strives for rationality for its own sake, not because of something that is supposed to result from it. Virtue can therefore only confirm one's rationality, which manifests itself in two spheres, in two types of activity: thinking and actions controlled by reason. The two dimensions of rationality have the so-called **virtues**, i.e. developed features of mind and character. None of them are inherent, but result from one's constant work on one's own thinking and behaviour. **Intellectual (dianetic) virtues** are the preferred features of the mind that can be worked out through learning. These include: wisdom, understanding, reason. All dianetic virtues are acquired by man based on knowledge and experience and are expressed in rational activity: "For the goodness or efficiency of a flute-player or sculptor or craftsman of any sort, and in general of anybody who has some function or business to perform, is thought to reside in that function; and similarly it may be held that the good of man resides in the function of man, if he has a function. Are we then to suppose that, while the carpenter and the shoemaker have definite functions or businesses belonging to them, man as such has none, and is not designed by nature to fulfil any function? Must we not rather assume that, just as the eye, the hand, the foot and each of the various members of the body manifestly has a certain function of its own, so a human being also has a certain function over and above all the functions of his particular members? What then precisely can this function be? The mere act of living appears to be shared even by plants, whereas we are looking for the function peculiar to man; we must, therefore, set aside the vital activity of nutrition and growth. Next in the scale will come some form of sentient life; but this too appears to be shared by horses, oxen, and animals generally. There remains, therefore, what may be called the practical life of the rational part of man."[29] On the other hand, **moral**

---

29 *Ibidem*, I, 1097b.25–1098a.6.

(ethical) **virtues** are the preferred character traits that can be worked out through constant repetition, habits. These virtues are not given by nature, although they cannot be realized independently of it. For nature gives us the opportunity to become morally virtuous people, but it is up to us and our activity to realize these virtues. These include: bravery, moderation, generosity, open-handedness, magnanimity, healthy ambition, gentleness, honesty, sense of humour, kindness, modesty, just indignation. In realizing these virtues, the practice of their constant repetition is important. Hence, a man becomes just while doing just deeds, becomes moderate when he acts moderately, becomes courageous when he acts bravely. And so, only one who can actively manifest both dianetic and ethical virtues has them: "And just as at the Olympic Games the wreaths of victory are not bestowed upon the handsomest and strongest persons present, but on men who enter for the competitions – since it is among these that the winners are found – so it is those who act rightly who carry off the prizes and good things of life."[30]

5.3 The principle of the *golden mean*

Rational activity, conditioning the achievement of virtue, is based on the knowledge and ability to apply the *principle of the golden mean*, testifying to Aristotle's love for balance and moderation. So what would the *golden mean* be? The philosopher believed it to be the preservation of the right average measure between excess and deprivation. Thus, the *golden mean* is the proper use of reason, consisting in controlling one's feelings and behaving in such a way as to never go to extremes. One who is impulsive and succumbs to emotions and impulses does not look for balance and moderation in their decisions but goes by way of extreme solutions. Aristotle gave numerous examples of the application of the *golden mean* principle in the second book of *Nicomachean Ethics*. In his opinion, courage is a virtue, or a preferred character trait developed by reason, the excess of which results in bravado, and insufficiency – in cowardice. Moderation (in the use of bodily pleasures) is a virtue that lies between licentiousness and asceticism. Generosity lies between extravagance and greed. Open-handedness, unlike generosity, concerns large sums of money and may fall into waste or

---

30 *Ibidem*, I, 1099a.4–7.

stinginess. Self-esteem, in turn, or justified pride is a virtue that can fall into excess – conceit, or insufficiency – humility. Is the use of moderation morally right for all attitudes? How does one evaluate theft, adultery, murder? How to treat such feelings as shamelessness, malice, envy? According to Aristotle, these are actions for which the search for moderation would not be morally praiseworthy, because they constitute evil in themselves. In the second book of *Nicomachean Ethics*, the philosopher writes: "Not every action or emotion, however, admits the observance of the golden mean. Indeed the very names of some directly imply evil, for instance malice, shamelessness, envy, and, of actions, adultery, theft, murder. All these and similar actions and feelings are blamed as being bad in themselves; it is not the excess or deficiency of them that we blame."[31]

5.4 Theory of friendship

The application of the *golden mean* principle does not only apply to the individual dimension of life, that is the development of virtues, but also to interpersonal relations. The issues of social ethics are raised in books VIII and IX of *Nicomachean Ethics*. Aristotle emphasizes that man is a social being, striving by its very nature to coexist with others and to create many relationships. In this case, the pursuit of moderation should determine the nature of interpersonal relations. Our reason advises us that, suggesting us to reject all extremes. One of them is hostility and the other is love. Thus, the path of moderation lies in nurturing friendly relations. Friendship becomes the highest social virtue conditioning the well-being and the feeling of happiness. In book VIII of *Nicomachean Ethics*, Aristotle distinguishes three varieties of friendly relations, depending on the nature and level of moral development of people entering into this type of relationship. Each friendship is a relationship of two people towards a certain good. The kind of friendship would depend on the nature of the desired good and on who owns the good. Aristotle distinguishes the following: 1) **Friendship based on interest. 2) Friendship based on pleasure. 3) Moral friendship**. At the first, lowest level of friendship based on interest, the goal is to achieve one's own advantage. These relationships are based on mutual utility. In Aristotle's

---

31 Aristotle, *Nicomachean Ethics*, II, 1106b.25–30.

belief, people who are mutual friends in the name of the benefits that result for them do not feel friendly for the other, but only in so far as a good thing results for each of them. In this case, the interest is related to the benefits of material nature, survival or improvement of living conditions. In their book *Ethics*, Peter Vardy and Paul Grosch say that in this case, an example can be a businessman who out of cold calculation maintains contact with a banker to ensure his kindness when applying for a loan. Such an interest-based friendship prevails where there is profit and money. This type of interpersonal relations, although commonplace, is not permanent. It only takes for a friend to lose wealth or influence and thus cease to be attractive as a source of our benefits. In another case, we may become affluent, and maintaining friendly relations based on material benefits will cease its purpose. Thus, if a friend is unable to give us the good we want, or the good has lost its attractiveness, then the friendship ends.[32] According to Aristotle, when the reason why people were friends disappears, friendship also disappears, if it existed only based on these purposes. For people who are only friends with benefit in mind, cease to be friendly when friendship ceases, since the subject of mutual friendship was not them, but their benefits.

The second type of friendship is not for material gain but one based on **pleasure**. Apparently, both sides are already economically independent enough to not need material support. They start to draw other good from relations with friends – pleasure. This type of friendly relationship is also anchored in the interests of both parties, but it is a bit subtler; it is not about the material but emotional sphere. Aristotle distinguishes three sources of pleasurable sensations: **intellect, beauty** and **carnality**. It's nice to interact with an intelligent, brilliant and well-read person, it's nice to see a beautiful face of a friend or experience bodily delights. It is enough to have one of these sources to make friendship possible. Is this type of friendship permanent? No, it isn't. Beauty passes, the body is aging, and the level of our friend's intellect and brilliance may stop satisfying us. The sources of pleasure pass away and so does the friendship. However, there is a kind of friendship that is not founded on self-interest: be it material or pleasure. It is the most valuable form of friendship, called **moral friendship**. It is only

---

32 P. Vardy, P. Grosch, *Ethics*, p. 42.

possible between people who are morally virtuous and only they can be friends in the absolute sense of the word. They wish each other well for the sake of a friend and not for the sake of the benefit they expect. Therefore, only those who can transcend their self-interest and never harm each other can create such a friendship.[33] The friend's well-being is more important to them than their own good. Only such friendship is permanent and consists in selfless care for the good of others. Aristotle describes this type of relationship as **friendship between good people**. However, this is an elite type of friendship, and therefore is rare. There are not many people who treat others as goals and do not want to live at the expense of others.

5.5 Man as zoon politikon

An important part of Aristotle's ethics is the conception of the social nature of man, connected with the theory of the state. The philosopher described his theory in *Politics*, recognizing that the natural pursuit of human beings is the need for association and community life. Man is a *zoon politikon*, a social animal, a creature of a political nature. The first manifestation of his instinctive pursuit of a collective life is a family that contains several types of relationships: husband and wife, parents and children, master and slave. Each of these relationships is natural in essence. It is nature that has established various degrees of talents in people, and so, the destiny of some individuals is to be masters, and others to be slaves. It is the birth right of some beings to be destined to submission and of others to rule. Several families put together form a village, a settlement, whereas the state (*polis*) is a developed association of settlements. Due to the fact that earlier forms of community life (family, settlement) arise in a natural way, the state is also a creation of nature. Aristotle distinguished three classes of citizens: affluent, very poor and representatives of the middle class.[34] The philosopher treated the first two groups negatively. In his opinion, the life of affluent people is 'contrary to nature' because they are not driven by the pursuit of happiness, but by the desire for unlimited profit and their propensity for luxury. In their strife for power, these people cannot submit to it themselves,

---

33 Aristotle, *Nicomachean Ethics*, II, 1234b.22–25.
34 Aristotle, *Politics*, IV, 1289b.27–31.

causing damage to state life. Therefore, the pursuit of wealth should not be an end in itself, but only serve to achieve a happy life. Similarly, the philosopher expressed negative opinions about poor people, ascribing to them the quality of humility, and the lack of intellectual capacity to govern the state. For lack of free time, poor people, doomed to physical labour, cannot improve morally and intellectually. In addition, they are materially dependent on others and do not have the autonomy that money gives. Representatives of the middle class, however, are the foundation of society. In their lives, they avoid the promiscuity typical of the rich and do not seek to cause revolutions, revolts, uprisings typical of poor people. It is this social class that should be the largest and thus strengthen the state's organization. So what should be the purpose of the state? Caring for the welfare of all citizens. The state should serve the common interests. Therefore, the best form of government is one that allows everyone the opportunity to do their best and live happily. Here Aristotle includes such forms of regime as monarchy, aristocracy and constitutional polyteia, in which the middle class maintains a balance of power between the upper class and the working class. Unfortunately, these regimes are prone to warping over time and instead of striving for the good of the whole, they aim only at the good of the ruling class.[35] These degenerate forms of power include tyranny (the rule of a despotic individual), oligarchy (the rule of the wealthy caring for their own gains) and democracy, in which the poor class is favoured to the detriment of the general interest.

6 Aristippus of Cyrene

Aristippus (435–366 BC) was a student of Socrates, the founder of the philosophical and ethical school called Cyrenaic. The name of the school comes from Cyrene, the birthplace of the philosopher, a Greek colony in North Africa. Aristippus was a propagator of **hedonism**, a notion that considered pleasure as the ultimate goal of all human endeavours. Unfortunately, none of the philosopher's writings have survived to this day, so we are left with indirect accounts. Aristippus' views are typical of both psychological and ethical hedonism. **Psychological hedonism** describes a certain mechanism

---

35 *Ibidem*, III, 1279a.22–31.

of human behaviour based on two types of stimuli: positive – pleasant, and negative – unpleasant. Thus, if we take any action, it is to achieve antici-pated pleasure or avoid suffering. Xenophon attributes the following words to Aristippus: "I count myself among the people who want to live the easiest and most pleasant way."[36] On the other hand, **ethical hedonism** recognizes maximizing one's own pleasure and minimizing suffering as a moral obli-gation. In Aristippus' opinion, pleasure is the only good worth seeking; it is the only state that possesses a positive value in itself. Unfortunately, this state is temporary, short-lived, fleeting and exists for as long as a stimulus lasts. What counts is only present pleasure, because only that is real. Past or future sensations are abstract. In addition, every pleasure has a sensual, carnal character. Every positive feeling, even the most subtle, spiritual or intellectual can be reduced to a physical experience. So what is happiness? It is the sum of the greatest possible number of pleasures experienced pres-ently and bodily. So the criterion of moral good is the personal satisfaction achieved in the present moment.

7 Epicurus of Samos

Most of Epicurus' writings (341–270 BC) are missing. Only three letters and excerpts of the work *On Nature* have survived to this day. Epicurus came to Athens from the island of Samos, and at the age of about 40 he founded his own philosophical school called the *Garden*. The inscription at the entrance to the school read: "Stranger, here you will do well to tarry; here our highest good is pleasure." Epicurus shied away from participation in social life, from active political activity, and he cared above all for the good of the individual. He is credited with the maxim: "Live in obscurity."

7.1 Happiness as the purpose of moral life

In the philosopher's opinion, **happiness** is the highest good, and virtue is not needed for itself, but in so far as it leads to one's happiness. In his *Letter to Menoeceus*, Epicurus wrote: "We recognize happiness as the original natural good; it directs all our desires or avoidance of something and we

---

36 Xenophon, *Memories about Socrates*, [in:] idem, *The Socratic Writings*, trans. J. Joachimowicz, Warsaw, p. 72.

always reach it as a goal (...)."[37] Epicurus believed that happiness consists in achieving a lasting and long-lived state of pleasure, which he did not understand in a vulgar, sensual way. In the third letter to his friend Menoeceus, the philosopher wrote: "When we say, then, that pleasure is the end and aim, we do not mean the pleasures of the prodigal or the pleasures of sensuality, as we are understood to do by some through ignorance, prejudice, or wilful misrepresentation. By pleasure we mean the absence of pain in the body and of trouble in the soul. It is not an unbroken succession of drinking-bouts and of revelry, not sexual lust, not the enjoyment of the fish and other delicacies of a luxurious table, which produce a pleasant life; it is sober reasoning."[38] Therefore, happiness is *aponía* or painlessness and spiritual independence understood as liberation from physical and mental pain. What would be the opposite of such an understanding of happiness? It is suffering, from which all people flee. Thus, Epicurus' ethics set a task analogous to modern psychotherapeutic methods, because its primary goal is the treatment of negative experiences. Porphyry describes the views of Epicurus as follows: "As there is no profit in the physician's art unless it cures the diseases of the body, so there is none in philosophy, unless it expels the troubles of the soul."[39] Therefore, happiness is not about chasing pleasures, but about being free from suffering. An indispensable condition for achieving this is the unbroken state of mind achieved thanks to independence from both the influence of the outside world and from one's passions. This state was referred to by Epicurus as *ataraxia* or the experience of spiritual peace, the inner silence resulting from freeing oneself from mental turmoil. *Ataraxia* is the serenity of the spirit associated with mental relaxation and inner balance, which can appear at any time and can be experienced directly. This spiritual peace can be illustrated by reference to the state of the sea during windless weather, where the smooth surface of the sea is not moved by any gust of wind. However, spiritual turmoil appears everywhere where two basic sources of mental suffering come to the fore: desires and fears.

---

37 Epicurus, *Epistula Tertia*; D. Laertius, X, 27, 129.
38 *Ibidem*, 131–132.
39 Porphyry, *Ad Marcellam*, 31.

7.2 Four-part remedy

Epicurus emphasized that freedom from suffering is conditioned by reaching their sources and mastering them with the power of one's own reason. If the first cause of human suffering are **desires**, then what should be done to reduce their impact on human life? First of all, Epicurus divided all human desires into 'natural' (related to the body) and 'unnatural' ones (related to the spiritual dimension of human existence). The former were then divided into 'necessary,' i.e. needed to keep one alive (e.g. the need for food, oxygen, sleep) and 'unnecessary,' i.e. those associated with body, but whose satisfaction is not directly related to the preservation of human life (e.g. the desire for bodily pleasure). The latter – 'unnatural' – ones, although they have a spiritual dimension, they result from pride and cannot be characterized as necessary (e.g. the desire for power, domination, immortality, interference in the course of history). In the belief of Epicurus, we should strive to satisfy our natural and necessary desires, while freeing ourselves from others or at least minimizing them. The second source of suffering is **fear** (*phobos*), hence the calm of the soul postulated by Epicurus means to free oneself from their power and achieve the state of **fearlessness** (*aphobos*). According to the philosopher, a man is primarily afraid of gods, death, the fact that he will not achieve his goals, illness and the accompanying physical pain. Overcoming these fears was to be aided by the so-called four-part remedy (*tetrapharmakos*), i.e. a set of four anti-anxiety principles: 1. Don't fear god. 2. Don't worry about death. 3. What is good is easy to get. 4. What is terrible is easy to endure. The first principle heals the soul based on the change of common ideas as to the gods' existence and interference in human life. They are not interested in human life, and so do not punish or reward. They exist only as role models, perfect beings that do not serve anything and do not affect human fate. The teachings of Epicurus put man before the gods in a relationship in which nothing should be expected of the gods. The gods live their own lives, parallel to the human world, but they have no contact with us in their existence. The purpose of the second principle is to tone down the second source of suffering, which is the fear of death. Epicurus emphasized the impossibility of man's spiritual existence after the death of the body and negated the concept of the soul as a separate, immaterial substance. Let us quote the philosopher's words from his *Letter to*

Menoeceus: "Accustom yourself to believing that death is nothing to us, for good and evil imply the capacity for sensation, and death is the privation of all sentience; therefore, a correct understanding that death is nothing to us makes the mortality of life enjoyable, not by adding to life a limitless time, but by taking away the yearning for immortality. (...) Death, therefore, the most awful of evils, is nothing to us, seeing that, when we are, death is not come, and, when death is come, we are not. It is nothing, then, either to the living or to the dead, for with the living it is not and the dead exist no longer."[40] In the case of the third principle, Epicurus recommends a minimalist way of understanding what is good. The primary value should not be pursuit of pleasure, but the enjoyment of the mere fact of existence. Life without suffering in itself should be a lasting source of joy. The last principle of the four-part remedy, according to which what is terrible is easy to endure, has a comforting character, minimizing the fear of physical pain. After all, suffering is the primary evil, and this is neither permanent nor acts with equal intensity. When there is fear of pain in our soul, we should console ourselves with the fact that intense pain will probably be short-lived, and long-term pain will not be so intense that it cannot be endured.

From the basic thesis of his ethics, Epicurus derives his teachings of social life. According to him, society is a community of individuals. Each individual, striving to achieve satisfaction, should not commit offenses against the public interest. Following the principle of pleasure should therefore be related to respect for justice. For people are not only afraid of gods and death, but also of other people. Hence, to subdue the fear of others, people conclude an agreement that they shall not harm one another. Observing this agreement is called justice. Man in social life should not inflict harm and not be injured.

8 Cynics

8.1 Antisthenes

The founder of the Cynic school was Antisthenes (444–368 BC), a student of Socrates, an Athenian half-citizen, son of a slave. In his *Lives and Opinions*

---

40 Epicurus, *Epistula Tertia*; D. Laertius, X, 27, 124.

of Eminent Philosophers, Diogenes Laertius wrote that Antisthenes has left as many as 10 volumes of his writings. Unfortunately, only two dialogues have survived to this day: *Ajax* and *Odysseus*, about the nature of virtues. There are two interpretations regarding the origin of the name of the school founded by Antisthenes. The first one refers to *Cynosarges* – the name of the gymnasium in which the philosopher taught, while the second one emphasizes the Greek word *kyne* – a dog, as Cynics showed preference for animal, dog life, detached from culture, tradition, customs, conventions, principles of good manners. They were abnegators, coming from the Athenian working class. They held no property, no positions, no social status. However, this lack was recognized by them as a value. They forged their material poverty into a philosophy of life. According to Antisthenes, the main goal of life should be to achieve virtue (*areté*), which is the only thing that has value in and of itself. This is the only thing that counts in one's life, everything else is irrelevant. Virtue can be acquired by anyone, regardless of gender, origin, race. However, if people consider other goods to be valuable, this is only the result of a convention and has no real value. Knowledge is not understood as erudite education, material goods hold no value. Nothing external matters, because man finds true value in himself. So what is this virtue? It is a developed inner strength of mind and character, consisting in independence of external goods and in the face of what fate brings us. According to Antisthenes, this virtue can be achieved by improving oneself in order to overcome one's own weaknesses, a work described as a **hardship** – *ponos*. Stoic hardships include ascetic physical and psychological exercises to overcome one's defects. The main disadvantage of man is his desire in general, and desire for pleasure in particular. Pleasant states result from sensory experiences, affluence, social status, reputation, etc. Antisthenes considered pleasure as evil, hence the idea of hardship was an idea for fighting this evil. Hardship is a conscious exposure to unpleasantness, annoyance, discomfort, pain to temper the spirit or to shape a specifically human nature. This is a work consisting in conscious exposure to negative experiences, maintaining the state of unmet needs. It is the practice of strong will to put up mental resistance, not giving in to one's fear of what is unpleasant and painful, and not chasing what is appealing and enjoyable. It is only through hardships that man can become a being internally free from passion, from striving to delight, from avoiding pain.

Freedom, after all, means liberation from the internal compulsion to chase anything and to become aware that pain, discomfort in life are nothing bad, and pleasures are nothing good.

8.2 Diogenes of Sinope

One of Antisthenes' students was Diogenes of Sinope (413–323 BC). Legend has it that Diogenes lived in a barrel, fed on what he received from people, dressed in rags and owned only a stick, a traveller's bag and a water cup, which he later discarded as unnecessary, because he saw a child drinking water with folded hands. The philosopher proclaimed the idea of self-sufficiency in that everyone should be enough for themselves, without the need for anybody or anything. His attitude has become a symbol of limiting one's life's needs to a minimum. The historian Diogenes Laertius in *Lives and Opinions of Eminent Philosophers* describes Diogenes as one who walked during the day around the Athenian agora with a lantern and called in the thick of the crowd: "I am looking for a human being." When asked about his impressions from the games, he would say: "There was a lot of crowd, but only few people." Typical of Diogenes' attitude was an event when King Alexander approached the sun-bathing philosopher and asked: "What can I do for you?" To which Diogenes replied that he might stand a little out of his sunshine. The philosopher was the first to describe himself as a cosmopolitan or citizen of the world (**kosmou polites**), denying the institution of the state as unnatural and artificial, derived only from tradition. Cosmopolitanism was the result rejecting the convention, and one of them was belonging to a particular *polis*. Diogenes – the cosmopolitan – thus accepted his alienation in his own community and acted not according to its laws, but according to the law of virtue.

9 Zeno of Citium

Zeno came from Citium in Cyprus (336–264 BC). In Athens, he founded a philosophical school, which he managed for 35 years. The name of the school – *Stoa* – derives from the Athenian portico painted in colourful frescoes – *stoa poikile* – in which the philosopher lectured. Apart from Zeno, the main representatives of the Stoic school included: Cleanthes (331–232 BC) and Chrysippus (280–205 BC). They created so-called Old

Stoa. What should the purpose of human life be? To proceed and live in accordance with nature. This is the first principle of Stoic ethics. Moreover, according to Zeno, nature is rational, since everything that exists has an internal plan (*logos*). Therefore, to live according to nature is to act rationally. This is the second principle of Stoic ethics. Nothing in harmony with nature and reason can be wrong. Zeno put a special emphasis on harmony in life. Man should base his actions on one principle, he should be consistent in thinking and in action, he should live in harmony not only with individual reason, but also with common sense. In the end, both natures (individuals and cosmos) are identical. In his *History of Philosophy*, Władysław Tatarkiewicz emphasizes the Stoics' pantheistic understanding of the world. The world is alive, rational, purposeful, and has a divine nature. God does not exist outside the world, but he is identical with it, because the divine element is *pneuma*, which permeates the whole world. Pneuma has a rational nature, it is a cosmic force that works in a necessary and purposeful way. Man's goal should be to recognize this strength and adapt to its laws. Whoever gains this life skill will become a virtuous man.

9.1 The sage's ideal

The ideal of a man should be a **wise sage** – rational, virtuous and happy at the same time. He is a man who has recognized his nature and the laws of divine logos and has accepted their effects. What does it mean to recognize one's own nature? It means to realize that man is part of the rational universe, and so his nature is also rational. So it is reason, not passions, that is predominant in human nature. Passions, or affects, are a disease of the soul; they are contrary to reason and incompatible with nature. Zeno developed a classification of feelings (*pate*) that become ingrained in a person through habits and make the human soul sick. The philosopher recognized four basic passions: sorrow, fear, lust and pleasure. Sorrow and pleasure refer to the present, while fear and desire involve the future. Especially sorrow – a spiritual paralysis – should never have access to the sage's soul, and so includes sadness due to someone's evil deeds, taking the form of compassion. One who has freed oneself from these feelings becomes a wise man. Zeno not only recommended to tone down one's passions (*metropatia*), but to eliminate them completely, extinguish them or reach the state of *apathy* (dispassion). After all, no affect is natural and serves any good. Apathy (*apatheia*) is the highest state of the sage, signifying the undisturbed spirit, an end in itself, the only goal to which all internal discipline should lead. Apathy is the result of rigorism, self-education involving constant opposition to forces that try to break it. Only thanks to this practice can a man gain internal freedom understood as freeing himself from the unnatural. Stoics used to say that even a shackled slave, when he becomes the master of his passions, is free, unlike his master, who has no rule over his emotions. On the other hand, a higher level of freedom was referred to as reasonable reconciliation with Logos, with what fate brings. Displaying the undisturbed spirit against everything that a person can meet. Accepting with peace both happiness and unhappiness, because everything is the work of **Logos-Providence**. Stoics depicted reconciliation with the Logos by means of the following allegory: a man is similar to a dog tied to a moving cart. If the dog is smart, he will run after the cart cheerfully, because he knows that even if he resists and howls, the cart will still pull him along. Thus, disaster and suffering befalling man, the passing away and death, are necessary elements of a rationally arranged world, which we should not oppose but accept with tranquillity. Only the wise man is free and other people are slaves. The wise man exceeds even the gods, because they are beyond suffering, and he is above suffering. Such a sage in perfect form is born once every 500 years. Beside the wise man, other people are fools, part of the mob.

9.2 The non-gradation of virtue

Zeno believed that virtue is one, indivisible and non-gradable. It can be achieved by a free man as well as a slave, a man and a woman. There are no intermediate stages between virtue and vice, rationality and foolishness. Either one is guided by reason and is virtuous in all respects, or is not guided by reason and is vile in everything. One cannot be a little intelligent and a little foolish. Therefore, people are divided into two groups: wise men and fools, good and bad. Even one who shows incomplete perfection is still unreasonable and regrettable; after all a man immersed under water one foot deep will drown just the same as the one who is way in the depths. Thus, one who goes along the path of virtue is still beyond virtue. One cannot, therefore, pursue good, righteousness and wisdom slowly and gradually. Those who do so are still depraved and foolish people. For the difference between the sage and the fool is not of rank but of quality. However, it should be emphasized that in their radicalism, the Stoics agreed to a certain concession and distinguished a particular subgroup in the group of fools, which would include people making progress. Those people are still fools, but they differ from others in that they make an effort to free themselves from the diseases of the soul. Moreover, the Stoics, recognizing virtue as the only good, and its opposite as the only evil, also distinguished an intermediate category regarding morally inert matters (*adiafora*). Good is reason, moderation, bravery and justice. These are the four essential virtues. Evil is foolishness, lack of self-control, injustice and cowardice. These are the four essential vices. Adiafora, on the other hand, is life and death, fame and disgrace, wealth and poverty, disease and health, positions, honours and beauty. These states, covered by the category of irrelevant things, are alien to man, and more specifically his nature, and are beyond his power. All these phenomena are fleeting and their lack or threat of loss cannot cause unhappiness. A wise man must be indifferent to them in the sense that he should neither desire nor despise them.

9.3 Social ethics

According to Zeno, society comes from nature, not from an agreement, because nature gave man social instincts. The consequence of this was the stoic postulate of participation in politics. Zeno used to say that the wise man would take part in public affairs if nothing disturbs him. The virtuous man will not live alone, for he is inherently a social being and a practical activist. In his opinion, even animals are characterized by an innate concern for offspring, and in man, this sense of relationship with others goes beyond their own children and involves all fellow men. Thus the Stoic postulates of kindness, friendship and charity are in line with human nature and, therefore, morally valid. Moreover, from the thesis about the existence of one cosmos, Zeno derived a theorem on the natural equality of all people, regardless of nationality, gender and social standing. He proclaimed the notion that all slaves are the same as free people, because both are just as subject to fate. Zeno dreamed of a country of wise men, in which all people and all nations would join together in a universal brotherhood.

10 Pyrrho of Elis

The creator of ancient ethical scepticism was Pyrrho of Elis in the Peloponnese (360–270 BC). The name of the direction he created derives from the word *skepticos*, i.e. doubting, observing. The primary source of knowledge about Pyrrho's views is the *Outlines of Pyrrhonism* by Sextus Empiricus, a sceptic living in the 2nd century AD, because, like Socrates, Pyrrho himself did not write anything and did not leave any works. According to the philosopher, the goal in life should be to achieve happiness understood as inner peace. So what would the source of anxiety be? Convictions about oneself, things, people and the world. In order to get rid of them and at least distance them, one should answer three questions: 1. What do things consist of? 2. How should we relate to these things? 3. How will we benefit from relating to them? According to Diogenes Laertius in the *Lives and Opinions of Eminent Philosophers*, Pyrrho, trying to answer these questions, came to the conclusion that "no thing stands out from among others." Therefore, nothing by itself should be called beautiful, ugly, just or unjust. Things only seem so to us, and our mistake is that we conclude what really exists from what we think exists. Man cannot reach the truth about anything and does not have any knowledge about the nature of the world. Thus, one cannot say anything certain about good either, because all knowledge, including moral knowledge, is – at most – probable. It is only a set of opinions, and opinions are irresolvable in terms of their truthfulness. We must, therefore, keep common sense and not take for granted what is only likely. Behaviour consistent with common sense does not require any knowledge at all. A given pattern of behaviour and a moral standard do not have to be absolutely right and we do not know if it is so; but it is enough for us that they are probably right. The consequence of realizing one's own cognitive limitations should be avoiding affirmative sentences and categorical judgements, or in a stronger version – abstaining from passing judgement in general, i.e. practising the *epoché* and refraining from speaking on any matter (*aphasia*). Only the *epoché*, i.e. the suspension of judgement, protects a man from inner turmoil and leads to happiness understood as inner peace. However, it is not easy to suspend judgement; it requires internal rigour, self-discipline, self-denial, continuous practice – a spiritual exercise, known as *askesis*. However, this is not an objective that can be achieved by the average person, but only by an outstanding individual.

2 Ethics in Ancient Rome

1 Neoplatonic Ethics

1.1 Philo of Alexandria

Philo of Alexandria (around 25 BC–40 AD), a Jewish thinker, representative of Neoplatonism, author of 40 works written in Greek. The essence of his ethical system was the conviction that moral good depends on renunciation, on escape from the material world. In his work, *De migratione Abrahami* (*On the Migration of Abraham*), the philosopher writes: "Depart therefore from the earthly parts which envelop you. O my friend, fleeing from that base and polluted prison house of the body, and from the keepers as it were of the prison, its pleasures and appetites. (…) But if you choose to collect again those portions of yourself which you have lent away, and to invest yourself with the possession of yourself, without separating off or alienating any part of it, you will have a happy life, enjoying for ever and ever the fruit of good things which belong not to strangers but to yourself."[41] The essence of Philo's moral theory is calling man to return to God, to let the human soul return to its divine primary rule. Through their corporality, people occupy one of the lowest places in the hierarchy of beings. The goal of a moral practice should therefore be to elevate man to the higher levels of ontic perfection. Ethics would be man's path to God. Philo distinguished three tiers of the ladder of beings, from the highest to the lowest: God, Logos and the material world. The material world exists because it is filled with a spiritual primacy that permeates everything and leaves nothing empty. Logos is a special bridge between God and the material world. For God permeates the world with the help of spiritual, immaterial forces or logos. The highest of the logos is the divine word; the other logos are forces – in accordance with the religious tradition – referred to by Philo as Angels. The set of these logos makes up an intangible world, not perceived sensually. Below this ontic level is the world of material creatures,

---

41 Philo Judaeus, *On the migration of Abraham 9–11*, [in:] H. Lewy, A. Altmann, I. Heinemann (eds.), *Three Jewish Philosophers*, New York 1960, pp. 109–110. Cited after: V.J. Bourke, *History of Ethics*, op. cit., p. 42.

created by God from matter, based on ideal patterns taken from the world of Logos. The bodily nature of human existence is the basis of its sinfulness. According to Philo, a man who survived even one day in the bodily shell is already impure. If the essence of moral life is to seek God, the basic component of the moral practice should be the renunciation of all that is flesh-related, all that separates man from God. Hence, the postulate of penance for bodily sins, ascesis, renunciation of the mundane world, spiritual purification of passions. Man is a bodily and spiritual being. His immortal soul is the carrier of the divine element, and it embodies everything that helps a person to rise higher. Unfortunately, it is enclosed in the body that pulls a man down. Therefore, the moral goal of man should be to 'escape the body,' free himself from the material prison and join a union with God. The condition for achieving this goal is the **practice of ecstasy (*ekstasis*)**, the spiritual act of leaving the body, a state devoid of thought, contemplation and insight. Ecstasy would be an act of God's grace, prepared by prayer and moral purity. The philosopher contrasts mystical ecstasy with both sensual cognition and theoretical thinking.

Philo is one of the predecessors of early Christianity, even though he did not write a single sentence about Christians. Nevertheless, his theory contains the main Christian theses: 1. Man is inherently a sinful being. 2. Logos is a word that comes from God and mediates between God and man. 3. Penance is to be done not by sacrificing animals, but by offering God one's own heart. 4. Man should despise earthly pleasures and mortify the flesh.

1.2 Plotinus

Plotinus (205–270 AD) came from Lycopolis in Egypt. He studied philosophy with Ammonius Saccas, founder of Neoplatonism and opponent of Christianity. At the age of 40, he moved to Rome, where he organized a philosophical school, which he ran for 25 years. The audience of this school were people belonging to the Roman elite: statesmen, politicians, doctors, and rhetors. One of Plotinus' disciples was the Emperor Gallienus himself. Plotinus left 54 dissertations, which his pupil Porphyry composed in six books, nine chapters each, which came to be known as *Enneads* (*Nines*). The first *Ennead* concerns ethical considerations, the second – physical ones, the third – cosmological ones, the fourth is a treatise on the soul, the fifth – on understanding, and the sixth concerns the highest categories. Plotinus said that the basis of all creation is the divine principle, the unspoken One, which is transcendent and supra-rational, and access to it is possible at rare moments of mystical ecstasy. One cannot assign any predicates to it, cannot apply to it any word from the human world, because it has no characteristic. The unspoken One is the cause of everything that exists.

In the *History of Philosophy*, B.A.G. Fuller writes that One emanates its own essence, distributes itself, until all possible forms of being are filled. Just as light flows from the sun, so does creation emanate from the divine element. However, when the light separates from its source, it immediately becomes something different and smaller. Plotinus sets up a whole ladder of gradual descent of the divine element into the physical, referred to as **emanation**. The first hypostasis – divine reason, which loses its unity, shifting into ideas and forms. The second hypostasis – the soul of the world, which is fragmented into individual souls. The third hypostasis – the physical and spatial world. Comparing the first divine element to light, Plotinus likens matter to gloom, darkness, a lack of light. Therefore, the transition from the One to the material world also embodies the descent from perfection to imperfection, from unity to multiplicity.

1.2.1 Reincarnation of individual souls

Let us begin our reflection on the ethical aspects of Plotinus' theory from reincarnation, related to the immortality of individual souls. Immortality of the soul is not an advantage; it only means infinite imprisonment in time, connected with the shift from one body into another. The human soul is the lowest immaterial emanation and can only emanate matter, i.e. body, which is something like a prison for it. In his *Enneads*, Plotinus writes that a soul entangled in a body is as if it were a 'sleeper' in comparison with a pure soul. Embodying the soul means its downfall and enslavement by the momentum that drags it into the ever-lower levels of creation. Thus, those who have brought their lives to a sensual and lustful level will incarnate after death into ever so lower beings or animals. Foolish people who have brought their lives to a vegetative level will reincarnate as plants. The souls of those who hurt others during their lives will be hurt in the next life, rich villains will be reborn into misery, and the murderers will be murdered in the next incarnation. The soul, however, may break this downward dash towards ever-lower 'worlds' and take the way back to the pure form, one liberated from matter, divine. Reincarnation is therefore not a desirable thing, but an ever-repeated 'nightmare in various aspects' from which the soul should free itself. Plotinus called for cleansing the soul of all that binds it to the body (*katharsis*), and the state in which the soul can break away from its bodily shell by means of spiritual exercise is called magnanimity (*megalopsychia*). The way to this end should be achieving **purifying virtues** that cleanse from material concerns and from interest in the body and sensory objects, and **sanctifying virtues** that make the soul similar to God. This is the practice for those who want to become God's children and happy people in life.[42] Let us point out that, according to Plotinus, the human soul can travel along not one but three paths: practising moral, cognitive or aesthetic effort, that is seeking and 'enjoying' the three highest values: – good, truth and beauty.

1.2.2 The problem of evil

If human existence shifts down, becoming more and more material and entrapped in the flesh, then human life becomes morally wrong. Vernon Burke in the *History of Ethics* emphasizes that in Plotinus' theory, the process of emanation, which is a descent into the imperfection of matter, necessarily means moving from good to evil. In this case, evil is interpreted as the impulse of the soul that has entered into its emanation or body in order to follow the path determined by the prompts of the body and the physical world. Thus, sin only appears when the soul 'gives birth' to the body, descends into it and finds itself trapped in the material world. Sin is the downfall of the soul, which does not mean absolute evil yet, because descent to the level of absolute evil would be the same as the annihilation of the soul itself. This fall means disappearance, the absence of good in the individual soul. In the first *Ennead*, Plotinus emphasizes that doing wrong means not doing good, it is to follow darkness, in which there is no more good.

---

42 Plotinus, *Enneada*, VI, 9, 2.

2 Roman Stoicism

2.1 Lucius Annaeus Seneca

Seneca (4 BC–65 AD) was born in Cordoba, Spain, which was then a
Roman province. He received a comprehensive education, learning philosophy from the most outstanding Roman philosophers. He held the title of
praetor and consul in Rome, and was the teacher of Nero. His greatest work
devoted to ethical considerations is 124 letters to a friend Lucilius, written
in the last three years of his life. The writings impress with the wealth of
topics, perceptions and reflections. In *Epistulae Morales ad Lucilium*, the
philosopher emphasizes that the main goal of human life should be to
achieve virtue. In his opinion, philosophy applies not to words but to things.
It is not intended to help spend a pleasant day or to kill boredom during lei-
sure. It creates and moulds the spirit, organizes life, directs action, indicates
what to do and what to avoid and sits at the helm and guides the course of
those who are tossed by the waves. Without it, no one can live peacefully
and no one is safe.[43] Therefore, all intellectual activity, all research should
be subordinated to virtue. It should be emphasized that Seneca was more
interested in practising virtue than in theoretically revealing its nature. Let
us emphasize that moral life is the practice of virtue, for truly miserable
and pitiful are those who always complain and think that the world order
is unsatisfactory, wanting to improve the gods' doing, instead of improving
themselves.[44] Hence, the goal of ethics would be man's work on himself,
because life is not good in itself, but a good life is.[45]

2.1.1 Fatalistic understanding of nature

Seneca is convinced that the world is governed by a material yet spiritual-
ized rational being. In his dissertation *Cuestiones naturales*, the philosopher
writes: "Do you want to call it fate? You would not be wrong. It is what
everything depends on, that of which all causes of things come from. Do
you want to call it destiny? Here you will be right as well. Its wisdom cares

---

43 Seneca, *Epistulae Morales ad Lucilium*, 20, 2.
44 *Ibidem*, 107, 12.
45 *Ibidem*, 70, 4.

for this world so that it runs an undisturbed course and fulfils its activities. Do you want to call it nature? You will not go astray, because from it everything that drives us is born with. Do you want to call it the world? You will not be in error. For it is all that you see: it is whole, joined with its parts, it sustains itself with its own power."[46] Seneca sees the material world as the body of Reason-God, and God as the basis of the world's existence. Fate is not a blind cosmic force; it is endowed with reason and consciousness. The philosopher thinks that everything in nature is subordinated to absolute necessity. The laws of destiny will not be moved by anyone's wishes, they will not give into compassion or pity. In *Epistulae Morales ad Lucilium*, the philosopher emphasizes that the order of the universe is guided by the eternal cycle of fate, whose first law is to adhere to what is decided. Fate is identical with God, who rules over all things and events. Nothing can change it. Therefore, a wise man is characterized by humbleness towards fate and patiently endures life's annoyances. Each of us should treat all misfortune as an opportunity for moral improvement.[47] Moreover, a wise man is one who has trust in his fate and has surrendered to its course. Let's recall the words of Seneca: "Fate leads those who want it, and pulls whoever does not."[48]

2.1.2 Virtue as submission to nature

According to Seneca, the basic requirement of ethics is the complete and voluntary surrender to nature. Happiness consists in living in harmony with nature and recognizing its rational necessity. However, there is no nature without God, or God without nature.[49] Therefore, the virtue consists in surrendering to the divine fate, recognizing its leading role in our lives. Requests and prayers are unnecessary in this case. In his *De Beneficiis*, the philosopher argues that one should never, under any circumstances, curse the fate, that one should not complain even when a fool or criminal becomes a dignitary and an honest man suffers humiliation because everything is ruled by Providence (***Providentia***). And Providence tells us that It

---

46 Seneca, *Questiones Naturales*, II, 45, 1–2.
47 Seneca, *De Providentia*, iv, 6.
48 Seneca, *Epistulae Morales ad Lucilium*, 107, 10.
49 Seneca, *De Beneficiis*, IV, 8.

is the one that checks the bills and the only one knowing each of our debts, repaying some of them in the long run, other in the short run, according to its means.[50] So, let us repeat, man should submit to divine necessity and use all misfortune to improve himself in moral qualities. Typical examples of virtues recommended by Seneca are: self-control, moderate desires, intelligent reflection and independence. Happiness does not depend on one's possession or sensory pleasures. For what is unstable on the outside cannot be the basis of a happy life. Therefore, its causes should not be sought outside of us, but within. It is true that Seneca does not postulate asceticism, despising wealth and rejecting pleasure. His recommendations concern only the intelligent use of these goods. Happiness is the preservation of an undisturbed state of mind and courageous enduring of what fate brings along. One of the conditions to achieve this state is to overcome the fear of death. Seneca argues that death is not terrible, it is not evil and it is not punishment. It is more an act of justice determined by the law of nature. Reconciling with death also means acquiescence to suicide, but only when the situation in which a man finds himself is detrimental to his dignity. Let us emphasize that Seneca did not propagate suicide, but allowed such possibility under certain circumstances; after all, in his opinion, avoiding death is the same disgrace as resorting to it.[51]

2.1.3 Social ethics

Although Seneca's concept is a typical example of the ethics of caring for oneself, yet this individualism is associated with performing tasks for the society and the state. The realization of these tasks is possible thanks to the social instincts that are inherent in all of us. In *De Beneficiis*, the philosopher wrote: "Take away social union, and you will rend asunder the association by which the human race preserves its existence."[52] Society is a natural institution, and people are a natural part of this one large whole. All men are brothers, and this brotherhood is the result of a rational nature. In *Epistulae Morales ad Lucilium*, Seneca declared that we are all members

---

50 *Ibidem*, II, 45, 1–2.
51 Seneca, *Epistulae Morales ad Lucilium*, 98, 16; 117, 22.
52 Seneca, *De Beneficiis*, IV, 18, 2.

of a great body. Nature created us as relatives because it created us from the same material and for the same purposes.[53] Therefore, the first duty of each of us should be to not harm other members of society, to nurture compassion and to love our neighbour. Seneca talks about charity (*beneficia*), which has a value of its own, and which should be the basis of interpersonal relations.

2.1.4 Condemnation of slavery

Seneca was one of the few Roman philosophers to ever condemn slavery. He emphasized that slaves are human and should have human rights. In *Epistulae Morales ad Lucilium*, he wrote: "They are slaves. Nay, rather they are men. They are slaves. No, comrades. They are slaves. No, they are unpretentious friends. Kindly remember that he whom you call your slave sprang from the same stock, is smiled upon by the same skies, and on equal terms with yourself breathes, lives, and dies."[54] Whereas, in *De Beneficiis* the philosopher emphasized: "It is a mistake to imagine that slavery pervades a man's whole being; the better part of him is exempt from it; the body indeed is subjected and in the power of a master, but the mind is independent." "It is, therefore, only the body which misfortune hands over to a master, and which he buys and sells; this inward part cannot be transferred as a chattel."[55]

2.2 Epictetus

Epictetus of Hierapolis (50–138 AD) was one of the greatest representatives of Roman stoicism, who had a significant influence on later philosophers. He was a Greek slave in the service of Emperor Nero. He later became a freedman and devoted himself to philosophical activity. Tradition has kept accounts that when Nero harassed Epictetus, he would say calmly: "You will break my leg," and when the leg indeed was broken, he said: "Did not I say that you would break it?" One of the students of Epictetus – Flavius Arrian – wrote his lectures in the form of eight books – *Diatribes*, and a

---

53 Seneca, *Epistulae Morales ad Lucilium*, 95, 52.
54 *Ibidem*, 47, 1–10.
55 Seneca, *De Beneficiis*, III, 20, 1.

textbook of ethics entitled *Enchiridion of Epictetus*. In the 5th century this
textbook was converted for the use of Christian monasteries. Epictetus
deliberately left no writings, considering direct contact with students and
a personal example as the best form of philosophical activity. He required
his students not only to show philosophical knowledge, but above all, put
it into practice. In *Enchiridion of Epictetus*, he asks: "But what do I desire?
To understand Nature, and follow her. I ask, then, who interprets her;
and hearing that Chrysippus does, I have recourse to him. I do not understand his writings. I seek, therefore, one to interpret them. So far there is
nothing to value myself upon. And when I find an interpreter, what remains
is to make use of his instructions. This alone is the valuable thing. But if
I admire merely the interpretation, I become more of a grammarian than
a philosopher."[56]

2.2.1 Happiness as a goal in human life

Epictetus divides philosophy into three parts, i.e. topoi: physics, ethics and
logic. The goal of all topoi is to bring people closer to a happy life. The first
topos explains the nature of the world and of man, what we have influence on and what does not depend on us. The initial words of *Enchiridion*
are: "There are things which are within our power, and there are things
which are beyond our power. Within our power are our judgments, will,
desire, aversion, and, in one word, whatever affairs are our own. Beyond
our power are our bodies, property, reputation, office, and, in one word,
whatever are not properly our own affairs. Now, the things within our
power are by nature free, unrestricted, unhindered; but those beyond our
power are weak, dependent, restricted, alien. Remember, then, that if you
attribute freedom to things by nature dependent, and take what belongs
to others for your own, you will be hindered, you will lament, you will be
disturbed, you will find fault both with gods and men. But if you take for
your own only that which is your own, and view what belongs to others
just as it really is, then no one will ever compel you, no one will restrict
you, you will find fault with no one, you will accuse no one, you will do
nothing against your will; no one will hurt you, you will not have an enemy,

---

56 Epictetus, *Enchiridion*, 49.

nor will you suffer any harm."[57] Therefore, learning about the world and getting to know oneself is a necessary condition for a happy life. One must learn the laws of nature; not to alter them, because that is not possible, but to humbly accept them and not to rebel against what is necessary. The wise man always follows a reasonable necessity. Peace of mind (*ataraxia*) can only be achieved by those who do not rebel against the course of events and submit to God's decrees. For, the only freedom which depends on us is spiritual freedom, understood as internal independence from what fate brings us. Epictetus calls for us to remember that we are only actors in a drama. If we are to play the role of a pauper in our lives, let us try and play this role as we should. The same applies to every other life role: a cripple, a ruler or an ordinary citizen. You are to merely play your part well; the choice of your role lies with someone else.[58] Thus, a slave who dispassionately and indifferently approaches experiences, the suffering and misery is freer internally than his master, who is a slave to his own passions and his own possessions. In spite of this, let us remind that Epictetus officially condemned slavery and called for no one to create situations for others they would not like to experience themselves. If a man would not want to be a slave, he should not tolerate slavery around him.

Another branch of philosophy, the second topos, concerns ethics understood as the philosophy of action. It informs about the proper conduct of man and his moral duties, which man should not only reflect upon, but most of all pursue. The third topos deals with how to develop not just any reasoning, but the so-called good mind and the associated right judgement (*orthós lógos*): "The most important topic in philosophy is the practical application of principles, for instance one saying that we ought not to lie: the second is that of demonstrations, for instance why it is that we ought not to lie: the third, that which gives strength and logical connection to the other two, for instance why this is a demonstration. For what is demonstration? What is a consequence? What is a contradiction? What is truth? What is falsehood? The third point is then necessary on account of the second; and the second on account of the first. But the most necessary,

---

57 *Ibidem*, 8.
58 Epictetus, *Dissertationes*, II, 5, 25.

and that whereon we ought to rest, is the first. But we do just the contrary. For we spend all our time on the third point, and employ all our diligence about that, and entirely neglect the first. Therefore, at the same time that we lie, we are eager to show how it is demonstrated that lying is wrong."[59]

2.2.2 Ethics as a moral self-improvement of the individual

Let us remind you that in the belief of Epictetus, virtuous life is a life in harmony with nature, whose laws are not within our power. Nature is permeated by God's reason and it is this reason that connects man with God. So man's desires regarding that which he cannot influence is the simple path to an unhappy life. Man cannot change fate, he cannot change the course of things. The only thing left to him is to change his attitude towards these things to achieve spiritual independence. If, then, we are caught up with misfortune, suffering, disease, poverty, then we should first make efforts to free ourselves from them, but if we fail, we should give up without murmur. Let's recall the words of Epictetus: "Demand not that events should happen as you wish; but wish them to happen as they do happen, and you will go on well."[60]

2.2.3 The postulate of universal brotherhood

Epictetus proclaimed that all people are divine children. Therefore, all people are brothers, regardless of their origin, social position, race. The philosopher propagated the idea of cosmopolitanism, the conviction that people are citizens of the world, recipients of the postulate of equality and brotherhood. All people are our fellow men and we should love every man like a brother. An act of brotherly love should concern not only those who wish us well and help us, but also the originators of our suffering: "(...) when beaten, he must love those who beat him as the father, as the brother of all."[61] It should be emphasized that Epictetus, like Seneca, exerted a huge influence on early Christianity, and paved the way for spreading the ethics of Jesus of Nazareth.

---

59 *Ibidem*, 52.
60 Epictetus, *Enchiridion*, 8.
61 Epictetus, *Dissertationes*, III, 22, 54.

2.3 Marcus Aurelius

Marcus Aurelius (121–180 AD) was the last great representative of Stoic ethics. He was a Roman emperor who ruled in the years 161–180 AD. His teachers were the well-known Roman rhetor Cornelius Fronto and the Stoic Junius Rusticus, who familiarized him with the views of Epictetus. The philosopher included his thoughts in a treatise written in the form of aphorisms and entitled *Meditationes*. In the views of Aurelius, full of pessimism and powerlessness, one can see a reflection of the fall of the Roman Empire. In *Meditationes* the philosopher wrote: "Human life is momentary, (…) the condition of the body is decaying, the soul spinning around, fortune unpredictable, lasting fame is uncertain. In a word, the body and all its parts are a river, the soul a dream and a mist. Life is warfare and a journey far from home, lasting reputation is oblivion."[62] The essence of Marcus Aurelius' thinking is fatalism and full humility towards fate: "Whatever may happen to thee, it was prepared for thee from all eternity."[63] The philosopher emphasizes that everything that happens, does so not only in accordance with the order of the universe, but also in accordance with the highest, divine justice.

Each of us consists of a body, soul and spirit, originating from God. It is thanks to the spirit that man can approach God, whereas death is his liberation. So what is good? Good is harmony, it is acting in accordance with the intelligent, divine laws of nature. What is evil? It is violation of the order and plan of the whole; it is a rebellion against the rational nature.

2.3.1 Principles of morally just conduct

The practical aspect of Marcus Aurelius' ethics is contained in his nine principles of just conduct: 1. Be willing to forgive your neighbour when he offends you because we all exist to serve one another. 2. Consider those effects of bad deeds that are unfavourable for the perpetrators. 3. Avoid moral judgements of others. 4. Remember your own vices. 5. Remember that you do not know the internal attitudes of your fellow men. 6. When an opportunity for anger presents itself, remember that you will soon

---

62 Marcus Aurelius, *Meditationes*, 4, 35.
63 *Ibidem*, 2, 17.

die. 7. We are really tormented not by the sins of others, but by our own judgements of others. 8. Remember that anger and regret may harm you more than the effects of others' actions. 9. Remember that courtesy and kindness for others are the best for both sides.[64]

3 Roman Eclecticism

3.1 Cicero

Marcus Tullius Cicero (106–43 BC) born in Arpinum, was recognized by ethics historians as the most outstanding representative of Roman eclecticism, combining the views of various philosophical schools. His most important works were devoted to ethical reflection, understood as a practical field. Cicero rejected Epicureanism in favour of Stoicism, which he combined with the ethics of Aristotle and Plato. In his opinion, the pursuit of happiness is a primary human goal based on the need to preserve life. However, spiritual happiness would be the fullest, most perfect form of our existence. Cicero's eclecticism involved the recognition of many methods propagated by ethics leading to this goal. The true path would be the sum of many paths that reveal various aspects of happiness. In his opinion, the first path leads to knowing nature, the second – to knowing the essence of man and his destiny, the third – to knowing virtue and its practical implementation.

3.1.1 The theory of good

Cicero emphasized that the word *virtus*, meaning virtue, is derived from the word *vir* (man). And the main feature of a man is endurance based on one's ability to despise death and pain. Virtue, then, is the persistent endurance of misery based on improving one's will and the attainment of spiritual balance and peace. Only through internal discipline and work on oneself can a man realize such qualities as temperance, courage, justice. However, man consists not only of a soul that he should temper, but also of the body. And although the body is less important than the soul, and the bodily goods are lower in hierarchy than the spiritual ones, care for the corporal aspect of our

---

64 *Ibidem*, 11, 18.

existence becomes necessary to achieve happiness. Hence, important factors
of a happy life should include: health, well-being, friends. In the fifth book
of his work *Tusculanae Disputationes*, Cicero wrote: "(...) There is a shame
in you that moderates lust, there is a protection of justice that is indispensable for the human society, there is a strong and lasting contempt for
death and pain in constant heroic deeds and imminent dangers. These are
all spiritual qualities. But also look at the sensual organs themselves: they
will seem to you, like the rest of the body, not only your companions, but
also the servants of virtue. If there are many things in your body, such as
strength, health, dexterity, beauty, you should put above pleasure, how can
you assess the soul's capacity? In these the greatest ancient scholars saw the
presence of something heavenly and divine."[65]

3.1.2 The law of nature, morality and the concept of good governance

According to Cicero, moral evil does not come from nature, but from
incorrect education and the emulation of bad examples. Also the social
scope of human attitudes is natural and is a manifestation of the laws of
nature. It is in accordance with them that man enters into relations with
other people and creates relationships: marital, family, social, culminating
in a state organization. The state is the culmination of community life, created in a natural way. Its purpose is to protect individual acquired rights,
implement the idea of justice, and protect citizens. According to Cicero,
moral obligations to other people result from the social nature of man. In
De Officiis, the philosopher described them as follows: 1. One should not
refuse a stranger in need of a meal or water, or advice if he asks for it. 2. One
should react when a stranger asks for help and do everything to prevent
evil. 3. However, one is not obliged to give up one's life for a stranger, or do
anything else that would harm one or significantly deplete one's resources.
4. Our help is first and foremost due to our family members.

However, we should remember that by fixing human relationships in
the laws of nature, Cicero did not assume that people are inherently equal.
Therefore, the goal of a state institution should not be to compensate for

---

65 Cicero, *Tusculanae Disputationes*, V, 30.

social inequalities or to eliminate differences. This thesis was used by Cicero to justify slavery as a phenomenon consistent with the laws of nature. Therefore, some people are naturally destined to be slaves, and acting for their liberation would mean acting against their nature. In the case of state systems, the philosopher divided them into positive and negative ones or socially degenerating ones. He condemned democracy as the mob's rule, and tyranny as the unlimited rule of an individual. He praised the republic and the mixed system, sharing power between the monarch, the aristocracy and the people. This was to express the idea of the so-called good governance, based on a universal agreement between all social groups.

4 Roman Epicureanism

4.1 Titus Lucretius Carus

The most outstanding representative of Roman Epicureanism, active in the 1st century BC, was Titus Lucretius Carus (c. 96–55 BC) – poet, artist, creator of the Latin literary language. However, the place of birth, activity and social position of this thinker are unknown. His poem *De rerum natura*, which contains an apologia of Epicurus' philosophy and stands against fatalism and the Stoic idea of fate, has been preserved to this day. No unrelenting necessity, destiny, or fate hovers over man. Gods do not exist and no divine forces interfere in the world and life of man. The human soul is material and is not eternal. It is a force typical of the human body and comes from 'grains of matter.' The soul is a psyche whose condition depends on the condition of the body.

4.1.1 Rational ethics

In his concept of ethics, Lucretius continues the Epicurean tradition that is alien to all mysticism. Man should strive for happiness, identified with the peace of mind based on rational activity (*ratio*). This reason, or more precisely, 'rational thought' should be the basis for improving oneself, aimed at achieving an ethical ideal (*ataraxia*). Therefore, the way to happiness is paved by a reasonable life, consisting in the resignation of unnatural and unnecessary needs such as: the accumulation of wealth, the desire for power, holding positions in public and political life or the pursuit of sensual delights. One must also control one's greed, envy, pride, sloth and

vanity. A determinant of a reasonable life should therefore be a change of
current behaviour and finding a new circle of friends – like-minded people
with whom friendship (*amicitia*) can be cultivated – the noblest form of
interpersonal relations. It is among one's friends that one may deepen one's
knowledge about the world, practise character together and cultivate such
values as brotherhood and solidarity. It is among friends who are far away
from public life that one can get the longed-for peace, based on a sense of
security and lack of fear.

4.1.2 Social agreement

Reflecting on the genesis of humanity, Lucretius described primitive people
as wild animals living in forests, who did not know fire, covered themselves
with skins stripped of wild animals. At this stage of development, humanity
did not know moral norms, laws or relationships. Lucretius believed that
the development of material culture was the cause of departure from the
original state. As a result, the elementary cell of social life was created –
family, which became the starting point for further development. Families
united into clans, and then into tribes based on concluded agreements
for greater security. These agreements became the seeds of future laws.
According to Lucretius, the state arose as a result of the evolution of relations based on social agreements. Thus, the state organization is the result
of a pact based on fulfilling mutual obligations.

5 Ethics of Early Christianity

5.1 Quintus Septimius Florens Tertullianus

Tertullian (160–240 AD) – one of the oldest Christian ethicists – was born
in Carthage in a pagan family and gained renown in Rome as a lawyer.
Approximately 195 AD he adopted Christianity and became its zealous apol-
ogist. He considered the purpose of his life to show the superiority of this
religion over other theological systems. After 20 years, however, he broke
up with the Church and joined the Montanist sect, characterized by strong
asceticism and moral rigour. His ethical views were strongly influenced not
only by the message of Jesus of Nazareth but also by the Stoics. Tertullian
opposed moral life to sensuality, religion to philosophy and Christianity
to paganism. In his treatise *De praescriptione adversus haereticorum*, he

wrote: "What then hath Athens in common with Jerusalem? What hath the Academy in common with the Church? What have heretics in common with Christians? We have no need of speculative inquiry after we have known Christ Jesus. When we become believers, we have no desire to believe anything besides."[66] In Christianity, therefore, there is no place for intellectual exploration and philosophical reflection. So where do we look for models of morally right conduct? Only in the Holy Scripture. It is in the Bible that man should find the ethical formula for life. Only in the Bible there is information about how to live best and how to "please God in ethical deeds." The reward for fulfilling God's will is eternal happiness, while the punishment for disobedience is eternal suffering.

5.2 St. Augustine of Hippo

St. Augustine (354–430 AD) – the most prominent Christian thinker of the patristic age – was born in Tagaste in Numidia. He was inspired by Cicero's writings to conduct philosophical studies; he was most impressed, however, by Plotinus' *Enneads*. He was a supporter of Manichaeism for 10 years. The fervent sermons of the Bishop of Rome St. Ambrose converted Augustine to orthodox Christianity. He included ethical issues in the following treatises: *Confessiones, De civitate Dei, De Trinitate, De beata vita*.

5.2.1 Theocentric eudaimonism

In the belief of Vernon J. Bourke – author of *History of Ethics* –, Augustine's ethics are based on theocentric eudaimonism. First of all, the main goal of every human being should be to achieve happiness (*beatitudo*).[67] It is not based on bodily delights, affluence, or even on inner perfection. Happiness is a spiritual union with God, being in closeness with God, understood as the highest good. Therefore, ethics should be understood as knowledge about how to approach God. In the eighth book of *De civitate Dei*, Augustine wrote: "(Ethics) concerning the chief good – that which will leave us nothing further to seek in order to be blessed, if only we make all our actions refer to it, and seek it not for the sake of something else, but for

---

66 Tertullianus, *De praescriptione*, 7.
67 V.J. Bourke, *History of Ethics*, p. 56.

its own sake. Therefore, it is called an end, because we wish other things on account of it, but itself only for its own sake."[68] Therefore, only love of God (*caritas*) stimulates us to ethical deeds, it is the basis of moral good. In *De spiritu et littera*, Augustine wrote that if we follow the commandments out of fear of punishment, and not from the love of justice, then we act like slaves, not like free people, and so we do not fulfil the commandment: "For no fruit is good which does not grow from the root of love."[69] There is a known saying of Augustine's: "Love, and do what you want" (**Dilige, et quod vis fac**). It does not mean that love to anyone justifies any of our actions. After all, love may favour, or glorify one specific person at the expense of limiting other people's interests. This sentence should be understood as follows: **Love God, and do what you will.** He who loves God will not be able to hurt anyone. He will show respect to every human being and will not prefer anyone.

5.2.2 *The concept of grace*

Such understanding of love (**caritas**), unlike earthly love, based on lust (**cupiditas**), can only be the result of God's grace. For love as the basis for morally good deeds comes not from man but from God. Therefore, good is a matter of grace. We become good people, not of our own will, but of the will of God, which we cannot earn. A man cannot become good by himself; moreover, this gift from God is given to him free. Grace is not granted for merit. If one could earn it, it would not be grace. The history of ethics shows the dispute between Augustine and Pelagius, who recognized the work of grace, but also stressed that man can earn it. According to Pelagius, grace understood as a special gift of the Spirit, is granted according to merit. Augustine, on the other hand, believed that no one was worthy of grace, otherwise it would mean the possibility of interfering in the will of God. Therefore, people are divided into those who received it and those who did not, even though no one deserved it. In Augustine's theory, recognizing grace as the basis of good causes that people are divided into good ones, i.e.

---

68 Augustine, *De civitate Dei*, VIII, 8. Cited after: V.J. Bourke, *History of Ethics*, p. 59.

69 Augustine, *De spiritu et littera*, XIV, 26. Cited after: V.J. Bourke, *History of Ethics*, p. 58.

those who do good that comes not from them, but from God, and evil ones, whose wickedness results from the lack of grace. The evil people shall be condemned, while the good ones shall be saved. The former belong to the 'City of Man' (*civitas terrena*), while the latter to the 'City of God' (*civitas Dei*): "Accordingly, two cities have been formed by two loves: the earthly one by the love of self, even to the contempt of God; the heavenly one by the love of God, even to the contempt of self."[70] Belonging to the 'City of God' is connected with another gift, which is the possibility of obtaining ethical knowledge in the act of enlightenment (*illuminatio*) – a supernatural cognitive state. In this type of cognition, the mind reveals the truth without reasoning, accepts some content just as its eyes see things (*visio intellectualis*). Why is this particular cognitive state important to moral life? Because in the act of illumination, man experiences moral truths, for which reason is helpless. For example, the Christian duty to love one's enemies is one such a truth. This is a supernatural principle, which human reason cannot reach on its own, and which the mind cannot comprehend.

5.2.3 Where does evil come from?

In Augustine's theory, God created the world out of nothing, with an act of free will. Therefore, everything that exists, if it does exist, is good, while evil is not real, it has no positive nature in ontic terms. In *De civitate Dei*, Augustine wrote that evil has no particular nature, and that the name itself does not mean anything but lack of good. Evil is not a substance, but a lack thereof, or a corruption of a substance. This is confirmed by the words contained in *Confessiones*: "So where is this evil? Where and how did it come into being? What is its root? What is its seed? Or perhaps evil does not exist at all? If so, why are we so afraid of and eschew what is not there? If our fear is unjustified, then it is certainly evil, because it tugs and torments our hearts without need. It is all the more evil since there is no object of fear, and yet we are afraid. Either what we fear is evil, or the very fact that we are afraid is evil. Where does this evil come from? Since God created all things, and being good, he created them as good. Being the greater and the highest good, he also created smaller goods, but after all,

---

70 Augustine, *De civitate Dei*, XIV, 28.

everything – both the Creator and his creations – is good."[71] Therefore, if evil is an absence of something, then people – beings endowed with free will – do evil when they fail to do good, or when they turn to the lesser good instead of the greater one. Can one be responsible for evil understood as a lack of good? Yes, because evil involves consciously not choosing to do good, turning away from good and higher goals. It is a conviction that man can do without God.

---

71 *Ibidem*, VII, 5.

3 Selection of Source Texts

THALES

1. Vouch for someone and misfortune is sure. 2. Remember about your current and absent friends. 3. Do not embellish the external appearance but have beautiful manners.
   (...)
5. Do not be simple-minded or malicious.
6. Beware of stupidity. 7. Love reason. 8. Speak of gods that they exist. 9. Think about what you are going to do. 10. Listen a lot. 11. Speak at the right moment. 12. Being poor does not make a reproach of the rich, unless your reprimand is very useful. 13. Do not praise a man who deserves contempt for his wealth. 14. Conquer by the power of convincing, not by violence. 15. Whatever you do well, assign it to the gods, not to yourself. 18. In youth, win happiness, in old age – wisdom. 17. You will gain memory through accomplishment, foresight through punishment, nobility through way of action, self-control through hardships, godliness through fear, friendship through wealth, persuasion through words, respect through silence, justice through common sense, courage through bravery, power through action and command through fame.

SOLON

1. Nothing beyond measure. 2. Do not judge; otherwise, a man caught in vice will hate you. 3. Avoid pleasures that give rise to sadness. 4. Pay urgent attention to the integrity of morals, which is more certain than an oath. 5. Seal words with silence and silence with the right moment. 6. Do not lie but tell the truth. 7. Take care of the appropriate things. 8. There is nothing more righteous than what your parents say. 9. Do not acquire friends too fast, and those which you get, do not push away quickly. 10. Learn the art of governing, learning to obey. 11. By demanding others to give you reports, also report to others. 12. Advise citizens on not what is the most pleasant but what the best is for them. 13. Do not be impudent. 14. Do not keep bad company. 15. Ask the gods for advice.

16. Respect your friends. 17. **Do** not talk about what you did not examine. 18. Be silent about what you know. 19. Be gentle to your neighbours. 20. Draw conclusion of obscure things based on clear ones.

DEMOCRITUS

1. (Vorsokr. B 41) Democrat. 7. Not from fear but from a sense of duty, refrain from your sins.
2. (Vorsokr. B 42) Democrat. 8. It is a great advantage to think of duty in misfortune.
3. (Vorsokr. B 77) Democrat. 42. Fame and wealth without reason are an uncertain acquisition.
4. (Vorsokr. B 98) Democrat. 64. The friendship of one wise man is better than the friendship of a host of fools.
5. (Vorsokr. B 99) Democrat. 65. Life is not worth living for the man who has not one good friend.
6. (Vorsokr. B 103) Democrat. 69. It seems to me that he who does not love is not loved by anybody.
7. (Vorsokr. A 169) Cic. De fin. V 8, 23. Democritian carelessness (securitas), which is like peace of the spirit (tranquillitas), called by him Euthymia – is happiness itself (vita beata) [...] 29, 87. This is the highest good he called on euthymia, peace, serenity of the spirit, and often athambia, that is a nature free of fear.
8. (Vorsokr. B 3) *Plut. De tranqu.* an. 2 p. 465. Whoever wants to live in peace of mind should not do too many activities in either private or public matters, and in everything he does, he should not take upon him things that exceed his strength and abilities... The right measure is more certain than excess.
9. (Vorsokr. B 7) Sext. Adv. Math. VII 137. We know nothing real about things, and the opinion of everyone is based on the inflow [of perceived images].
10. (Vorsokr. B 108) Democrat. 75. Whoever seeks good will find it difficult, but evil comes to one who does not search for it.
11. (Vorsokr. B 145) Plut. De puer. educ. 14 p. 9 F. The Word is a shadow of the deed.

12. (Vorsokr. B 170) Stob. Ecl. II 7, 3. Both happiness and unhappiness dwell in the soul.
13. (Vorsokr. B 181) Stob. Ecl. II 9, 59. A better teacher of virtue will be the one who uses encouragement and convincing words than the one who applies law and coercion. In hiding, sins the one whom only law abstains from commitment a vile deed.
14. (Vorsokr. B 182) Democrat. Ecl. II 31, 66. Beautiful objects are wrought by study through effort, but ugly things are reaped automatically without toil.
15. (Vorsokr. B 214) Stob. Ecl. III 5, 25. The brave man is not only he who overcomes the enemy, but he who is stronger than his pleasures.
16. (Vorsokr. B 247) Stob. Ecl. II 40, 7. To a wise man, the whole earth is open. For the native land of a good soul is the whole earth.
17. (Vorsokr. B 248) Stob. Ecl. IV b. 1.33. The law wants to bless people's lives. However, it can only do it to those people who want to experience it.
18. (Vorsokr. B 249) Stob. Ecl. IV 34. Civil war is a disaster for both sides, because for the winners and for the losers result the same losses.
19. (Vorsokr. B 255) Stob. Ecl. IV 48. When the rich conquer themselves and them who have nothing, give loans, help them and show kindness, there is pity, solidarity, fraternity, mutual help, consent of citizens and so many other benefits that nobody would be able to enumerate them.
20. (Vorsokr. B 283) Stob. Ecl. IV 33, 23. Poverty and wealth are names for lack and superfluity. That is how it is that the one who feels the lack is not rich, and the one who does not feel the lack is not poor.

PYTHAGORAS
1. (Mullach, *Fragm. Philos. Graec.*) Aureum Pythagoreorum Carmen.

Above all, worship the gods, as the law commands. Have an oath in holy respect. Also, honour the famous heroes and deities of the underworld by offering them due sacrifices. Respect parents and relatives of their relatives and choose from among others those who are of the most outstanding virtue. Listen to their voice when they kindly advise you or do a favour to you. Do not be discouraged by friends because of their minor failings – as much as it is possible. This is because possibility is close to necessity. Remember what is right. Above all, try to overcome: first of all, the stomach and sleep, then pleasure and anger. Do not do anything shameful to others either with anyone or by yourself in secret. Most of all, be ashamed of yourself. Then follow justice, both in words and deeds. Try to get used to doing everything carefully. Know that everyone's destiny is to die. Earn wealth sometimes, then again abandon it. With the misfortunes the gods affect the mortals, bear peacefully and without a murmur the part destined to you by fate. You can also use remedial measures as much as you can. Know, however, that fate does not give too much of them to the good ones. You will hear much human talking, both good and bad. You, however, should not listen to them with admiration, nor allow them to get you away from your goal. If someone says something wrong, listen with indulgence. And what I tell you now, keep in every matter: let no one, whether through words or through deeds, make you say or do something that would not be better for you. Think about it before you do something, so that you will not be ridiculed. For to speak or to do without prior reflection is the property of a reckless man. Do what you will not have to regret later. But do not do anything you do not know. Learn first everything that can be useful to you. In this way, you will spend your life in the greatest joy. Do not neglect your health concerns. Keep moderate in eating, drinking and exercising. Speaking of moderation, I mean everything that will not cause you suffering later. Get used to the simple, not sumptuous way of life. Avoid everything that arouses jealousy. Do not be generous where you do not have to, like someone who is unaware of what is good and decent, but also do not be a miser. In all things, moderation is the best solution.

Do what will not hurt you, but before you do anything, think first.

Let sleep not rest on your tired eyelids before you pass through your deeds of the past day: what did I do wrong? What have I done and what have I left undone with my duties? From the beginning to the end, examine all the deeds in succession, and repent with the repentant of the bad, and rejoice in the good. These things you have to exercise hard, to think about them, to love them. They will testify for you on the way to the divine virtue – a witness, who has implanted in our soul the idea of the four, which is the source of the everlasting nature.

Put also hands to work, but first pray to the gods to bring your work to fruition. If you stick to these principles, you will know the properties of the nature of immortal gods and mortal people – and what is the difference between them and what they share with each other. You will learn the divine laws in nature and how similar it is in every part of it. And neither will you expect what is not possible, nor will it be hidden from you what can be fulfilled. You will learn how people experience misfortune, the perpetrators of which are they. The poor! Since they neither see good nor hear it, although it is close to them! And there are few who can be saved from misfortune. This is the fate of mortals who blind their thoughts, they roll like discs in this and that direction and countless is their suffering. A dangerous companion is the spirit of opposition that is inherent in them and hindering them from hiding. Do not wake it but avoid it.

Father Zeus! Of how many misfortunes you would have freed everyone, if you would reveal to people what nature is in all of them! You, however, be of good thought. Divine is a pedigree of mortals. The holy nature reveals and shows them everything. And if you understand something of it, you will keep my teachings. And you shall heal your soul and free yourself from torment.

Refrain from forbidden food. Know, that this is part of the cleansing rites and the liberation of the soul from evil. Consider all this. For the highest guide, choose reason, the gift of gods. When you disconnect with the body and fly in the ether – space – you will become immortal, immaculate as God and not be subject to death.

PLATON

1. *Symp.* 203 B–204 C. [Socrates reports his conversation with Diotima].
   When Aphrodite was born, the gods attended a feast, and among them was Abundance, the son of Caution. When they had eaten, Poverty was there to beg for something, because there was everything galore, and she stood near the door. Abundance, having drunk nectar (because there was no wine then), went to the garden of Zeus and there he fell asleep, heavily drunk. Poverty wanted, as it was poor, to have a child with Abundance, she lay down beside him and thus she conceived Eros. And that is why Eros became a companion and servant of Aphrodite, because he was begotten on her birthday, and by his nature he is already a lover of beautiful things, as Aphrodite was also beautiful. And since he

was the son of Abundance and Poverty, this fate fell to him: above all, he is an eternally poor man; he is far from having delicate features and beauty, as he seems to many people; he is clumsy and looks like a freak, and barefoot, and homeless, without bedding he sleeps on the doorstep somewhere or near the road, a roof is never over his head, because he is of his mother's nature. But like his father, he chases what is beautiful and what is good, he is courageous, a serious hunter, he always devises a way, he tries to reason, he cannot cope, and he philosophizes his whole life, a terrible wizard, poisoner or sophist; neither god nor man. And one day he lives and flourishes, then he dies, and arises again from the dead, because he is of his father's nature. And whatever he gains, he loses again, so that he neither suffers nor lacks in abundance. And he is in the middle between wisdom and stupidity. Because that's the way it is: no god philosophizes or desires wisdom – he has it; no other wise creature philosophizes. The fools also do not philosophize and none of them wants to be wise. Because it is all misfortune in stupidity that a man is neither beautiful nor good, nor wise, but he thinks it's enough for him. If a man thinks that something is not missing from him, will he want what, in his opinion, he does not lack?

"My Diotima," I say, "and who in that case deals with philosophy, if not wise nor stupid"?

"This," she says, "even the child will understand that those who are something intermediate between one and the other." To those also belongs Eros. Because wisdom is undeniably beautiful, and Eros is the love of the beautiful; therefore, Eros must be a lover of wisdom, a philosopher, and a philosopher in the midst of it remains between wisdom and stupidity. And this is also his origin. For his father is wise and rich; and the mother is silly and poor. So, this is the nature of this spirit, my Socrates. And if you imagined Eros differently, no wonder. Of what you say, I think, that you took the object of love to be Eros and not love itself. And that is why Eros seemed to you so attractive. Yes, the object of love is really beautiful, subtle, finished and perfect. But what is loved, looks different, o yes, as I told you.

2. *Symp.* 208 E–209 C [Socrates is referring Diotima's lecture], "But there are also people," he says, "who prefer to fertilise their souls, those whose souls are fuller of seed than the body: the seed that is to

be born in the human soul." And what should be born in the soul?
Reason and all other bravery. This seed is really sown by creators of
all kinds, and the performers are those who have an inventive gift. And
the greatest reason – he says – is he who should rule the country and
the home, whose name is self-control and justice. So, he who is full of
this seed from his youth, has a divine thing in his soul. And when he
approaches his age, he desires to beget and create, and I also think he
starts to walk here and there and look for beauty that would fertilize
him. Nothing ugly will he fertilize. And he prefers the beautiful bodies
than the ugly ones, because he has much semen, and more willingly he
meets souls beautiful, brave, healthy, and he enjoys the most when he
meets one joined with the other. Then such a man begins to talk a lot
about prowess and what a stout person should a man be and what he
should make, and he begins to educate him. He met what was beautiful
and started to commune with it. Then what it longed in him for a long
time and was only a seed begins to radiate and fertilize both when they
are together with each other, and when they are only connected through
memory; and whatever they spend, they cherish and conceal: so that,
without comparison, a stronger union starts to connect them, than if
they had children otherwise and a more enduring friendship is between
them, just as their children are more beautiful and less subject to death
than anyone else.

ARISTOTLE

1.*Eth. Nicom.* II 5, 1105b 18–1106a 10. In turn, we need to consider
what ethical prowess is. Now, because there are threefold phenomena
in the mental life: passions, abilities and permanent dispositions, ethical
prowess must belong to one of these three kinds. Passions are my lust,
anger, fear, courage, envy, joy, love, hatred, longing, jealousy, pity –
everything that is accompanied by pleasure or pain; I call this ability,
thanks to which we can experience the above-mentioned passions, so
that we are able to [e.g.] be angry, grieve, or pity; finally, I call what is
lasting dispositions, thanks to which we relate to passions in the right
or wrong way, for example to anger we refer wrong, if we do it in a
violent manner, or one which is too weak, and well – if we do it in moderation, and similarly in relation to other passions.

Passions, therefore, do not include any ethical advantages or disadvantages, because they do not call us good or bad ones because of passion, but they call us in this way because of ethical virtues or flaws; further, because of passion, we do not obtain praise or reprimand [...] For the same reasons, they also do not belong to the ability, because they are not called good or bad, they do not praise nor rebuke because of the very ability to experience passions taken in the absolute sense. And further: we have capabilities from nature, and virtues and ethical faults are not innate to us, as mentioned above. If then virtue does not belong to passion or to ability, then there is nothing else but the fact that they belong to permanent dispositions.

2. *Eth. Nicom.* II 1, 1103a 13 nn. There are two types of valour, one of which are dianetic virtues, and the other – ethical values or virtues. Both the creation and the development of dianetic qualities are usually the fruit of science and therefore they require experience and time; ethics, on the other hand, is acquired thanks to habituation, which results in their name (etikai from ethos), slightly different from the word "habit" (ethos). It also follows that none of our virtues is inherently innate; because nothing of what is inborn can be changed by being accustomed; thus, for example stone falling downwards by nature cannot be taught to climb upwards, even if someone tried to get it used to it, throwing it upwards countless times; you cannot get fire accustomed to falling down or to anything else – against its nature. So, virtues do not become our share either thanks to nature or against nature, but by nature we are only able to acquire them, and we develop them in ourselves through our habits.

3. *Eth. Nicom.* II 6, 1106b 36 nn. Thus, ethical prowess is a permanent disposition for a certain kind of provision, which consists in maintaining the right measure for us, which is defined by reason, and in a way that would be described by a sensible person. This is the average measure between two errors, i.e. between excess and deprivation; and further: the average measure, in as much as these errors do not reach what is appropriate in the experience of passion and in the proceedings, or beyond this boundary, when ethical prowess is found and takes the right measure. Therefore, because of the substance and the definition

qualifying its essence, ethical prowess is something lying in the midst, but when it comes to what is best and good, it is something extreme.

However, not all proceedings and not all passions allow a medium measure; for the very names of some of them indicate that they are a wicked thing, such as joy from the failure of others, shamelessness or envy, and from among the ways of conduct: adultery, theft and murder; all these and similar passions and practices are reprimanded because they are themselves wicked, not their excess or deprivation. One can never act properly within them, but he must always err; in relation to this kind of thing, good and evil are not in this [e.g.], with which woman, when or how to commit adultery, because doing any of it is an erroneous thing. Similarly, there is an opinion that moderation, excess and deprivation exists in relation to injustice, cowardice or promiscuity; there would be moderation in excess and scarcity, excess of excess and deprivation of deprivation. However, as there is no excess or lack of moderation or bravery, because the centre is somewhat extreme, so in respect of those with patency there is neither moderation nor excess nor deprivation, but no matter how one commits it they are always wrong, as there is no moderation in abundance or scarcity, and there is neither excess nor scarcity.

4. *Eth. Nicom.* II 8, 1108b 10–33. There are three kinds of dispositions, two of which are flaws (the first is due to excess, the second is due to scarcity), while the other, namely the preservation of the right measure, is an advantage; all these dispositions mutually contradict each other, as both extremes are in opposition to the centre and mutually to each other, and the centre is the opposite of both extremes; as if something which is equal to another, is greater than something smaller than it, and smaller than something larger than it, such persistent dispositions that hold on to the centre mean excess in relation to scarcity, and scarcity in relation to excess – both in experiencing passions as well as in proceedings. For a courageous man is to a coward a bold man, but to a bold he is a coward; and similarly, a moderate man seems to be dissolute to an insensitive man, but insensitive is he to a dissolute; generous to a greedy seems prodigal, but to a thriftless man – a greedy man. That is why the people who are standing on the edges always move the person who stands in the middle towards the opposite end and call

[e.g.] a brave man: coward – impudent, and impudent – coward, and similarly in other cases. In such a way, the mutual opposition to these lasting dispositions is more opposed to each other's ends than to each of them in the middle. For their distance is greater than each of them from the middle, as is the greater distance of what is greater than a certain size, from something smaller than it, and something smaller than a certain size, from something it's bigger than them both from something equal to that size. And further: some extremes are somewhat similar to the inside, for example boldness to bravery, and extravagance to generosity; the extremes, on the other hand, are completely unlike each other.

5. *Eth. Nicom.* I 6. V 15, 1097b. 5 nn. Let us go back to the good we are looking for and the question of what it can be. It turns out that in every kind of action and in every art it is something else: something else in medicine, something else in the art of commanding – and similarly in every other art. So, what is good in each of them? Is this the goal of everything being done? Well, this is health in medicine, victory in the art of commanding, a house in architecture, in other arts something else again, in every action and in every undertaking – this is the goal; the purpose of everything being done. If, then, there is one common goal for all possible activities, then it is probably the highest good that can be achieved by action, but if there are more goals, then they probably are them.

Our considerations have reached the same result using a different path; but we must try to explain it even closer. In view of the fact that the goals – as it turns out – are different and that some of them, such as wealth, flute and any tool, we choose for other purposes, it is clear that not all are final goals. The highest good, however, seems to be something final. So, if there is only one thing that is the ultimate thing, then it would be what we are looking for; if there are more such things, then one of them would be what we seek, which is the most important. What we strive for ourselves is called something more final than what we aspire to for something else; we also call to a greater degree what is never sought for anything other than the things that are pursued for both themselves and for something else. Hence, it is absolutely final what is always pursued for it and never for something else.

It is happiness, which – according to popular opinion – corresponds to this term; for happiness always strives for it, and never for something else, but honours, pleasures, reason and all boldness, we also want for (we would like to have each of these things, even if we did not come to any of them), we do it but also for happiness, in the conviction that thanks to these things we will be happy. Happiness, however, is not to strive for the aforementioned things or for anything else except for itself.

6. *Eth. Nicom.* I 4, 1095a 15 nn. As for the name of this [supreme] good, most people have almost universal consent; for both uneducated people and people with higher culture see them in happiness, and they think that being happy is the same as living well and having a good life; to the question, however, what happiness is, the answers are divergent and uneducated, the commonalty defines them differently than the wise. For some, happiness means something beyond reality and visible things, such as pleasure, wealth or honours, others see it in something different, and often, even one and the same man sees different things (being sick, he sees happiness in health, being poor – in wealth); being aware, however, of their ignorance in this respect, people admire those who make high-level claims being upon their comprehension. Some of them finally come out with the view that, in addition to the aforementioned multitude of goods, there is still another good, good in itself that makes them all goods. Well, all these views to consider is a vainly struggle, it is enough to deal with those that are the most widespread or seem to have some justification.

7. *Eth. Nicom.* I 7, 1098a 10 *im.* If the peculiar function of man is the action of the soul according to reason or not without reason; and if the specific function of a man and an ethically standing human is the same as that of a certain type, such as the function of a zitherist and a great zitherist, and in all cases at all, because only the higher one joins the function caused by bravery (areté) (it is the function of the zitherist to play the zither, as the function of good zitherist to play well). If so, and if we consider a certain type of life to be a kind of human function, namely the operation of the soul and acting in accordance with reason, and the specific function of a brave man, the same action performed in a particularly good way; if at last everything is done well, which is done in a manner consistent with the requirements of its own bravery;

if then all this is so, the highest good of man is the action of the soul in accordance with the requirements of its bravery, and if there are more types of this bravery, it is in accordance with the requirements of the best and the highest of its kind. And this is the life that has reached a certain length. For one swallow does not make a summer; neither one day nor a brief time gives bliss or happiness to man.

8. *Eth. Nicom.* I 8, 1098b 20 nn. Happy is he who lives well and who is successful, because we have almost described happiness as a kind of good life and success. It turns out further that our definition of the concept of happiness contains all the qualities that were demanded for it. For some see it in ethical prowess, others in reason, others in some kind of wisdom; still others think that the essence of happiness are the things mentioned or one of them combined with pleasure or without pleasure, there are also those who also include external well-being here. Some of these views have many ancient representatives, other few but very famous; probably none of them are completely wrong, but everyone has a certainty at least in some respects or even to a large extent.

As for those who see happiness in ethical prowess or in some of its kind, our entire term agrees with this view: they belong to the bravery of the actions that follow it. However, it is probably a considerable difference whether we see the highest good in the possession itself, or in use, permanent disposal or in operations. For the disposition, though it exists, can do nothing good, as in a sleeping or otherwise inactive person; however, it cannot be done; because it will work out of necessity, and it will work well. And as in Olympia, the most beautiful and the strongest ones are not those crowned, but those who take part in the games (as there are winners among them), so those who are good and morally beautiful in life also become those who work.

At the same time their life is pleasant in itself. For the enjoyment of pleasure belongs to the spiritual life and everyone enjoys the things he loves, such as a horse for a horse lover, a spectacle for a spectator, and a just thing for a lover of justice; generally speaking, what is in agreement with courage for a lover of courage. These things that please the general public are incompatible with each other, because they are pleasant not by their nature; the things that make the lovers of what is morally beautiful are pleasant, they are pleasant by nature. Here, it is necessary to act in accordance with the rules of ethical valiancy, which is therefore pleasant both for the above-mentioned people and in itself. The life of these people, therefore, does not need pleasure as an additive, but it contains this pleasure in itself. In addition to what has already been said: it is not an ethically brave man who does not enjoy beautiful deeds; for no one shall be called righteous who does not enjoy a just behaviour, nor generous is a man who does not enjoy a generous manner; similarly, this is also the same in other cases. If so, then acting in accordance with the rules of ethical prowess is probably pleasant in itself. In addition, it is also good and beautiful, and it is in the highest degree, if a noble man thinks of these things correctly; and he thinks as we said.

So, happiness is the highest good and morally the most beautiful, and the supreme pleasure, and these are not separate things, as the inscription in Delos says: "What is the most righteous is the noblest, health – the best, and the most pleasant thing: to achieve your goals." All these qualities are included in the best activities, these are the activities or one of them, namely the best; they are, in our opinion, happiness.

It turns out, however, that happiness – as we have already mentioned – cannot do without outside goods; after all, it is impossible, or at least not easy, to perform morally beautiful deeds, being deprived of adequate resources. For many things happen – as if with tools – thanks to friends, wealth or political influences; however, there is a lack of certain goods, such as good birth, successful children or lack of beauty, which spoil happiness.

9. *Eth. Nicom.* V 1, 1129b 12 nn. If a man transgressing the law was unjust, and the one who held the law was just, it is clear that everything in accordance with the law is in a sense just; for what is established by the legislative authority, is lawful, and everything that falls under this concept is called just. Laws regulate everything, heading towards what is beneficial for everyone (or for the best) or for those who wield power either because of bravery or because of something else; so that in one sense we call just that which in the commonwealth is a source of happiness and contributes to its maintenance and to maintaining everything that is made of it. The law requires you to perform acts of bravery (e.g. do not abandon your position, do not run away, do not drop your weapon), as acts of moderation (e.g. do not commit adultery, do not

commit rape), as acts of gentleness (e.g. do not beat or insult) – and similarly with regard to other ethical advantages and disadvantages, the first to prohibit others; and all this makes the law well, if it is well formed, and worse – if it is hastily patched up.

Thus, justice is understood as identical to ethical perfection, but ethical perfection not in itself, in an absolute sense, but in relations with other people. And that is why it sometimes seems that justice is the greatest of virtues and that it is not dawn nor afterglow which is worthy of such admiration; and hence the proverb:

In the justice of all virtues is a flower.

Moreover, justice is identical to ethical excellence in the full sense of the word, because it is the application of ethical excellence in practice; it is identical to perfection, because whoever has it can do it not only in relation to himself, but also in relation to others; for many people know how to deal with their own affairs in accordance with the rules of ethical prowess, but they cannot do it in relation to their neighbours. Therefore, it seems accurate what Bias said, that power "shows what kind of person one is," because whoever has power remains, a result of this, in relations with other people and is a member of the community. That is why justice, the only one among virtues, seems to be "someone else's good," because it also involves the attitude towards others, as it does what is useful to others: be it to the ruler or to fellow citizens. Therefore, the worst is one who does wrong not only towards himself, but also towards his friends; the best is not a man who reveals his ethical prowess towards himself, but who does it in relation to others; since this is a difficult task.

Thus understood justice is not part of ethical prowess, but it is all the valour; likewise, contrary to this justice, injustice is not part of wickedness, but all the wickedness itself. And what the difference between ethical prowess and justice is in this sense results from the above arguments; it is one and the same permanent disposition, but appearing in a different form: considered because of the attitude to others, is justice, and considered in an absolute sense, is ethical prowess.

EPICURUS OF SAMOS

A Letter to Menojkeus. Diog. Laert. X 122–135. May the young man not neglect philosophy, and may not the old man feel unable to study it any more. For it is neither too early nor too late to begin to take care of the health of one's soul. Who therefore claims that the time for philosophizing has not come to him yet, or that it has already passed, he is similar to one who claims that the time has not come for happiness or that it has already passed. Therefore, both young and old should philosophize: the latter so that they feel young, remembering the good they were favoured with in the past, the former to be fearless in the face of the future in spite of their youth, like the elderly. Therefore, constantly strive for what happiness can bring to us; who has happiness, has everything that can be at all possible, and whom fortune has missed, will do everything to achieve it.

Try to follow what I have been advised and think constantly about it, remembering that these are the basic principles of a glorious life. Above all, consider the deity an indestructible and happy being according to the universal image of the deity and do not attribute to him qualities that would oppose his immortality or be against his happiness. Make sure that your concept of the deity includes everything that can preserve its immortality and happiness. The gods, however, exist, and their cognition is an obvious fact; however, they do not exist in a way as the crowd imagines; crowd imaginations are variable. Ungodly is not the one who rejects the gods worshipped by the crowd, but the one who shares the opinion of the crowd about the gods. However, the opinions of the crowd are not based on conceptual ideas, but on false guesses. Hence, the belief that the gods send the greatest misfortunes to evil, and that the greatest benefits are good evidence. Completely focused on their own virtues, they regard the gods as similar to each other, different from them – as alien.

Try to get used to the idea that death is nothing to us, because all good and evil are connected with feeling; and death is nothing but a complete deprivation of feeling. Therefore, this irrefutable conviction that death is nothing to us makes us appreciate the mortal life better and it does not add an endless time, but it knocks out the desire for immortality. In fact, there is nothing terrible in life for one who has realized well that stopping living is nothing scary. The fool is the one who says that we are afraid of death, not because it causes us pain when it comes, but because we are concerned about its expectation. Because indeed, if a thing does not disturb us with its presence, then the anxiety caused by its expectation is completely unfounded. So death, the most terrible disaster, does not concern us at all, since we exist, death is absent, and as soon as death appears, then we are gone. Death, therefore, has no relation to either the living or the dead; the former do not apply and the latter does not exist. However, the crowd shuns death as the greatest evil, or again wants it as an end to the misery of life. But a wise man, on the contrary, does not renounce his life, nor is he afraid of death, for life is not a burden to him, and he does not consider non-existence completely evil. Just as he does not choose food that is more abundant, but tastier, he does not mean the longest persistence, but the most pleasant one. And the one who calls for a young man to live beautifully, and an old man to beautifully end his life, is naive, not only because life is always desired by both, but rather because the care for a beautiful life – it is not different from the care for its beautiful end. Much worse, however, is he, who said that it would be better not to be born or after birth, as soon as possible, to cross the gate of Hades (Theognis 425, 427).

If he says it seriously, why does not he leave his life? And it would be easy for him, if he had such a firm intention. If, however, he wants to make a joke, then the joke is out of place because it is no joking matter.

It should be remembered that the future is not entirely ours, nor is it completely independent of us; with that in mind, we will not expect it to be fulfilled, nor will we lose hope of its possible fulfilment.

You also need to realize that among our desires some are natural and others imaginary, and among the natural ones, some are also necessary, while others are only natural. Among the necessary, one can distinguish those that are necessary to happiness than those that are necessary to the peace of the body and finally necessary to life itself. A clear view of these matters will allow any choice and avoidance of the body and peace of the soul in favour of the health, and this is the goal of a happy life. However, all our activity is going to be free of suffering and anxiety. And once we manage to achieve all this, the anxiety of the soul soon disappears; for the living being feels no longer the need to strive for anything that would lack, nor will he seek anything else to complement the good of the soul and of the body. Because then we only feel the need for pleasure when we experience pain because of its lack; but when the pain does not bother us, we do not need any pleasure then. Well, that's why we say that pleasure is the beginning and purpose of a happy life. For this is, in our opinion, the first and natural good and the starting point of all choice and avoidance; we finally return to it, when we refer to the feeling as a criterion of all good.

And precisely because it is the first and the innate good, we do not chase after all pleasure but often give up many ones; we do so especially when we expect them to suffer more pain. And it happens that many problems are higher than pleasure, which happens when, after experiencing long-lasting pain, we expect to experience greater pleasure. Therefore, all pleasure is good because of its own nature, but not everyone is worthy of choice; and similarly, all pain is bad, but not every pain should be avoided. In any case, you need to carefully examine it in terms of usefulness and harm, because sometimes it happens that good is taken for evil and vice versa, evil for good. We consider moderately to experience the greatest good, not because we have to be satisfied with a small one, but because we learn how to deal with anything when poverty hits us, in the belief that those benefit the abundance of good most are those who desire it the least, and what is natural is easy to achieve, and what is imagined is difficult to gain. Simple food gives us as much pleasure as expensive feasts as soon as the painful feeling of hunger is removed. Barley bread and water give the greatest pleasure if you eat it hungry. Therefore, the habit of a simple and low-cost life provides good health and activates various life needs, and when after a long break one sits down at a set table, these pleasures are better enjoyed; and ultimately this makes us fearless against the tides of fate.

When we say that pleasure is our supreme goal, we do not mean the pleasure of debauchery, nor sensual pleasure, as said by those who do not know our knowledge or disagree with it, or by those who they interpret it wrong. The pleasure that we have in mind is characterized by the absence of physical suffering and the lack of anxiety of the soul. For it is not the drinking and associated carousing, or contact with beautiful boys and women, or fish and other delicacies, which provide an exquisite table, that give us a pleasant life, but sober reason, inquiring the reasons for all choice and avoiding and rejecting the idle guesses that are the source of the greatest afflictions of the soul. Of all this, wisdom is the beginning and the greatest good, and consequently it is even more valuable than philosophy; for it is the source of all other virtues. It teaches us that you cannot live pleasantly, if you do not live wisely, beautifully and justly, and vice versa, you cannot live wisely, beautifully and justly, if you do not live pleasantly. However, virtues create together with a pleasant life a natural unity and a pleasant life is inseparable from them.

For whom would you more value than a sage, who godly worships the gods and does not fear death at all, and understands what the ultimate goal of nature is, and understands that the highest good can easily be obtained, and the greatest evil either lasts for a short time or makes only light pain; from omnipotent destiny, which some philosophers introduce as supreme power over everything. I laugh, saying that certain things arose out of necessity, others by chance, and some thanks to us, because necessity excludes all responsibility, and the case is changeable, and our will does not depend on any external authority; therefore, its conduct is accompanied by both praise and reprimand. Indeed, it would be better to recognize the mythological fairy tales of gods than to become a slave to the naturalists. Mythology, in fact, allows at least the possibility of atoning the gods worshipped by it, whereas destiny is inexorable. Also, the sage does not consider the fortune as a deity, like the common people do (because in the action of the deity there is no place for chaotic disorder), nor for a variable cause. He does not think that fortune gives people good or evil to provide them with a happy life; he thinks only that he provides them with the ingredients of great good or great evil. He believes that it is better to be unhappy with a reason than to be happy without it. It is better, of course, when a fair judgement in his action does not expect help from fortune.

So, think carefully about these issues as well as those linked. Meditate day and night. Alone and with someone who thinks similarly, and you will not experience anxiety when asleep or awake, and you will live among people like a god. For a man who lives in the realm of indestructible values is quite unlike any mortal being.

CICERO

1. *De amicitia* 8, 26 n. So when I often thought about friendship, the most remarkable question seemed to me whether friendship is desirable because of weakness and powerlessness, so that everyone who renders and receives benefits could obtain from others what he cannot obtain himself, or whether such exchange of services is truly attached to friendship, but the reason is different – more important, beautiful and derived from nature itself. Because it is love, or araor, where the name of friendship also comes from – amicitia is a factor encouraging to establish friendly relations. After all, the benefits can often be obtained from

those whom one gains pretending to be a friend and whom respect is shown due to circumstances, whereas in real friendship there is nothing invented and nothing successful, and whatever is there is true and voluntary. Therefore, it seems to me that friendship comes from nature rather than from need, rather than from the inner tendency of a man, connected with a feeling of love, rather than from the calculation of how much benefit will result.

2. *De amicitia* 23, 88 n. So the nature of a man does not tolerate solitude and always tries to find for himself some kind of support, which is the most pleasant in the form of the most beloved friend.

But although nature reveals to us what it wants, what it demands and what it requires, I do not know how it is that we are not listening to it. For the manifestations of friendship are different and manifold, from where arises many causes of suspicion and offences, and it is the duty of a wise man to avoid them, to soften them and to endure them.

3. *De amicitia* 26, 100. Virtue, virtue, I say, Gaius Fannius, and you, Quintus Mousius, both associates and sustains the relation of friendship. For in it all consent is contained, in it there is constancy, in it is irreplaceability. When it rises and reveals its radiance, when it perceives and recognizes the same radiance in the other, then it approaches it and takes over what it sees in it.

4. *De amicitia* 5, 19. Well, it seems to me that we were born to live in order for a bond to exist between all of us, the closer we are to a particular individual, the closer the bond. 6, 20. Friendship is nothing else but compatibility in all divine and human matters, connected with mutual kindness and love.

5. *De amicitia* 7, 23. If you have removed the bond of kindness from this world, then neither a house nor a city will stand, and even the cultivation of the land will not last.

6. *De amicitia* 13, 47. You get the impression that they want to remove the sun from the world – those who remove friendship from life – and there was nothing better and nothing more pleasant given to us from the immortal gods.

7. *De fin.* III 19, 63. Hence again, it is natural that mutual kindness among people is also natural, so that man – precisely because he is a human being – cannot look at another person as something foreign to himself. For as among the body parts, some have been created for

themselves, for example eyes and ears, while others also help in using other parts, such as legs and hands, some wild animals were created only for themselves, while some of them otherwise. We will mention here a snail living in a large shell and another creature that emerges from its shell; because it protects the snail, it is called the guard of the snail, but when it withdraws, the shell closes, which looks as if the creature was giving warning signs. Ants, bees and storks also do something for other creatures, but the relationship existing between people is much closer. Therefore, they are naturally disposed to gathering and living in a community.

SENEKA

1. *Letters* 2–5. If you want to experience happiness, ask the gods that none of their wishes would come true. They are not good things which they want to shower you with. There is only one good, which is the principle and foundation of a happy life: to rely on oneself. However, this cannot be achieved if one is afraid of hardship and does not count what is neither good nor bad. Since it is unlikely that one and the same thing would be wrong once, and good for the second time, once light and easy to bear, and the second time frightening. Toil is not good. So what is good? Not being afraid of the toil.

   Therefore, I would rebuke the ones who are occupied with vain things. Those who are torn again towards the noble work, the more they will apply to them, the less they will be able to overcome and restrain, the more I will praise and cry out: "You are much better now! Arise, breathe in and climb up that hill, if you can, in one breath." For precious souls, toil is refreshment. So you do not need that, according to this old... [example] of your ancestors, you choose, what you would like to happen to you and what your wishes are. In general, it is ugly for a man abducted by the most cherished intentions to continue teasing the gods with requests. What do you need prayers for? Make yourself happy on your own. You will do it if you understand that good is what has virtue inside, and evil is associated with anger.

2. *Letters* 48, 2–3. No one can live happily if he only considers himself and everything is turned to his own advantage: it is necessary to live for others if you want to live for yourself. This bond that connects us with

other people, and results in some common law for the entire human race, when it is diligently observed it can be very helpful also for practising these closer relations of friendship which I have mentioned above. He who has much in common with people, will have everything to do with a friend.

3. *Letters* 70, 4–5. Not always, as you know, life should be prolonged. For good is not life itself, but a beautiful life. That is why the sage lives as much as he should live, and not as much as he can live. He will wonder where to live, with whom, how and what to do. He always considers what life should be like, not how long. When, however, he encounters many troubles and circumstances disturbing his calmness, he moves away.

4. *De vita beata* IV 1–4. One can also describe our good differently, that is to express the same content in other words [...] One time, you can extend and dilute this term and concentrate and constrict it on another occasion. The content will remain the same if I say: "The highest good is the spirit that despises every contingent thing, and of virtue itself derives joy," or: "The highest good is the invincible power of the spirit, tried in the heat of experiences, gentle in action, imbued with a great love for people and concern for those with whom one meet in life." One can also give a definition that we would call a happy man for whom only good or evil is a good or evil soul, who nourishes nobility, finds enjoyment in virtue, which cases of fate neither raise nor break, which does not recognize a greater good than that which he can afford himself, which he considers the only delight to be – a contempt for lust. If more variants suit someone, they may express the same guiding idea in a different form, as long as it does not violate or distort its essential content. What does prevent us from saying that a happy life is when the spirit is free, sublime, fearless, steadfast and inaccessible to fear, inaccessible to lust? There is only one good for him – righteousness, one evil – infamy, and everything else for him is worthless, which neither increases nor decreases happiness in life, and their gain or loss takes place without benefits, as well as without damage to the highest good. On such grounds, constant gaiety and deep joy, flowing from deep sources, must accompany the established strength of spirit, whether someone wants it or not,

because such a spirit rejoices in its own goods and does not desire any goods greater than those that it has inside. Why should he put these goods on a par with the miserable, wicked and fleeting impulses of a miserable body? On the day someone enjoys pleasure, he will also experience suffering. You see yourself, what grim enslavement a man will enter, if he is agitated by pleasure and pain, the two of the most penniless, and at the same time cruel tyrants. You need to escape serfdom to gain freedom.

5. *Meditations* II 17. The length of human life – a point, the being – fluid, perception – unclear, whole body – rot, soul – vortex, fate –puzzle, fame – uncertain thing. In short, everything related to the body is a river, related to the soul is a dream. Life – is a war and a temporary stop on a journey, a posthumous memory – forgetfulness. So what can be used as a refuge? Only one thing: philosophy. And it relies on keeping our demon without blemish and damage, that he may be stronger than pleasure and suffering, that he may do nothing without consideration or in a false and hypocritical way that he will not desire anything from anyone. To accept all events and fates as they were coming where he came from. And above all, that in every position he would expect death with comfort in the conviction that it is nothing but the decomposition of elements from which every creature consists. If, however, the constant transformation is not terrible for the elements itself, why do you fear the change and disintegration of all? After all, this is happening in accordance with the laws of nature. And nothing is wrong which is in harmony with nature.

6. *Meditations* XII 36. You were, o man, a citizen of this great country. Why would you care whether it were five or a hundred years? What is in line with the law, is equal for everyone. What then is terrible in this, when you are removed from the frontiers of the state by not a tyrant, not a just judge, but the nature that has introduced you in it? Just like a praetor removes from the stage the actor, the same one who engaged him. "But I did not play five acts, only three." "Well, but in life there are three acts which form the entire art. It was designated by the one who assembled the group and now dissolves it. You did take part neither in the first nor in the second act. So go gently. For he is also gentle who releases you."

SAINT AURELIUS AUGUSTINE

1. Fragm. Philosophical works of St. Augustine, b. IV

Everything that exists is good and comes from God – the highest good. The Supreme Good, than which there is none higher, is God; for this reason He is immutable good, and therefore truly eternal and truly immortal. All other goods are from Him alone, but not of His substance. For that which is of His substance is identical with Himself, but the things which He has made are not what He Himself is. It follows that, if He alone is immutable, all the things which He has made, inasmuch as He has made them out of nothing, are mutable. For He is so almighty, that even out of nothing, that is out of that which is utterly non-existent, He can make goods both great and small, both celestial and terrestrial, both spiritual and corporeal. However, because He is also just, He has not made equal to that which He has begotten of Himself those things which He has made out of nothing. Inasmuch, therefore, as all goods whether great or small, whatever be their rank in the hierarchy of beings, can have existence only from God, and since, moreover, every nature is a good in so far as it is a nature, every nature can be only from the supreme and true God; because all goods, even those which, while not supremely good, are close to the Supreme Good, and likewise all goods, even the very least, which are remote from the Supreme Good, can be only from the Supreme Good itself. Therefore every spirit, even the mutable, and everybody is from God, that is every created nature; for every nature is either spirit or body. Immutable spirit is God; mutable spirit is a created nature, yet superior to body. Body is not spirit except in so far as the wind is called spirit, in a different sense, since, although it is invisible to us, its force is felt and is strong. Now on behalf of those who, not understanding that every nature, that is even spirit and everybody, is naturally good, are perturbed by the wickedness of spirit and the mortality of body, and who therefore attempt to introduce another nature of wicked spirit and mortal body which God has not made, we are of opinion that our explanation can be adapted to their understanding as follows. For they admit that every Good can have existence only from the supreme and true God, an admission both true and affording a sufficient corrective to their error, if they but choose to examine it. For we

Catholic Christians worship God, from Whom are all goods whether great or small, from Whom is every limit whether great or small, from Whom is every form whether great or small, from Whom is every order whether great or small. For certainly the more things possess of limit, form, and order, the better they are; but the less things possess of limit, form, and order the less good they are. These three therefore, limit, form, and order – not to mention the innumerable qualities which can be shown to pertain to these three – these three, then, limit, form, and order, are, so to speak, goods possessed in common by the things which God has made, whether spirit or body. It follows that God is above every limit, above every form, above every order of the created universe; and this, not by spatial position, but by ineffable and unique power, since He is the source of every limit, every form, and every order. Where these three are great, there are great goods; where they are small, there are small goods; where they are absent, good is absent. Again, where these three are great, there are great natures; where they are small, there are small natures; where they are non-existent, there is no nature. Therefore every nature is good. Consequently, when we seek the source of evil, we must first of all investigate the nature of evil. Evil is nothing else than the corruption of the limit, the form, or the order of a nature. Hence, a nature that has been corrupted is termed evil, for obviously an incorrupt nature is good. But even a corrupt nature is good inasmuch as it is a nature; to the extent to which it has been corrupted it is evil. Now it can happen that a nature which ranks higher because of its natural limit and form is still better, even when corrupted, than an in corrupt nature which occupies a lower rank with reference to its natural limit and form. Just as in the judgement of men, which, in evaluating properties, depends upon external appearances, gold even when impure is better than pure silver, and silver even when impure is better than pure lead, so too in the case of the more powerful natures, that is spiritual natures, a rational spirit, even when corrupted through its evil will, is better than an incorrupt irrational nature; and any spirit whatsoever, even when corrupted, is better than any incorrupt body; for a nature which, when associated with a body gives it life, is better than a nature to which life is given. But however corrupt a created life-giving spirit may be, it can give life to a body; and for that reason it is better, even though corrupt, than the body, although it be incorrupt. If corruption should remove from corruptible things all limit, all form, and all order, no nature would remain; and for this reason every nature which cannot be corrupted is supremely good, as God is. But every nature which can be corrupted is nevertheless a good thing, for corruption could not harm it except by removing and diminishing what is good.

All selected texts have been translated by Andrzej Fudała and Dave Fowler, based on the book by Jan Legowicz (ed.), *Ancient Philosophy of Greece and Rome. Selected Texts from the History of Philosophy*, PWN, Warsaw 1968.

Bibliography

Source texts

Aleksandryjski F., *Pisma*, trans. L. Joachimowicz, vol. I, Warsaw 1986.

Aristophanes, *Clouds*, in: Aristophanes, *Comedies*, trans. J. Ławińska, Wroclaw 1991.

Aristotle, *Great Ethics, Eudemean Ethics*, trans. W. Wróblewski, Warsaw 1977.

Aristotle, *Nicomachean Ethics*, trans. D. Gromska, Warsaw 1982.

Augustine of Hippo, *Spirit and Letter*, trans. W. Eborowicz, Warsaw 1977.

Augustine of Hippo, *Confessions*, trans. Z. Kubiak, Warsaw 1987.

Borussica A.R. (ed.), *Aristotelis Opera, Graece-Latine cum Scholiis*, vols. I–V, Berlin 1831–1870.

Cicero M.T., *Philosophical Writings*, trans. W. Kornatowski, J. Śmigaj, Z. Czerniakowa, Warsaw 1960–1963.

Epictetus, *Diatribes*, trans. L. Joachimowicz, Warsaw 1961.

Kirk G.S., Raven J.E., and Schofield M., *The Presocratic Philosophy*, PWN, p. 421.

Heidegger M., *Letter on 'humanism'*, trans. J. Tischner, [in:] idem, *Build, Live, Think*, Essays, Warsaw 1977, p. 119.

Krońska I., *Socrates*, Warsaw 1989, p. 76.

Lucretius T.C., *On the Nature of Things*, trans. G. Żurek, Warsaw 1994.

Marcus Aurelius, *Considerations*, trans. M. Reiter, Warsaw 1984.

Philo Judaeus, *On the migration of Abraham 9–11*, [in:] H. Lewy, A. Altmann, I. Heinemann (eds.), *Three Jewish Philosophers*, New York 1960, pp. 109–110.

Plato, *Symposium, Euthyphro, Defense of Socrates, Crito, Phaedo*, trans. W. Witwicki, Warsaw 1984.

Plato, *Republic*, trans. W. Witwicki, Warsaw 1991.

Plotinus, *Enneads*, trans. A. Krokiewicz, vols. I–II, Warsaw 1959.

Porphyry, *Life of Pythagoras*, trans. J. Gajda-Krynicka, Epsilon, Wroclaw 1993, pp. 11–24.

Seneca L.A., *Moral Letters to Lucilius*, trans. W. Kornatowski, Warsaw 1961.

von Arnim J. (ed.), *Stoicorum veterum fragmenta*, vols. I–III, Leipzig 1903–1905.

Witwicki W., *Introduction to the Euthyphro dialogue*, [in:] Plato, *Dialogues*, trans. W. Witwicki, PWN, Warsaw 1984, p. 174.

Xenophon, *Memories about Socrates*, [in:] idem, *The Socratic Writings*, trans. J. Joachimowicz, Warsaw, p. 72.

Studies

Ahbel-Rappe S., Kamtekar R., *A Companion to Socrates*, Oxford 2006.

Armstrong A.H. (ed.), *Classical Mediterranean Spirituality*, Crossroad Publishing, New York 1986.

Becker L.C., Becker C.B. (eds.), *The Encyclopedia of Ethics*, New York 1992.

Boas G., *Rationalism in Greek Philosophy*, Baltimore 1961.

Bourke V.J., *History of Ethics*, trans. A. Białek, Torun 1994.

Brinton C., *A History of Western Morals*, New York 1955.

Diels H., *Die Fragmente der Vorsokratiker*, Berlin 1912, VIII ed. Diels H., Kranz W., Berlin 1956.

Dittrich O., *Geschichte der Ethik. Die Systeme der Moral vom Altertum bis zur Gegenwart*, Aalen 1964.

Ebert Th., *Sokrates als Pythagoreer und die Anamnesis in Platons Phaidon*, Mainz-Stuttgart 1994.

Fuller B.A.G., *History of Philosophy*, trans. Z. Glinka, Warsaw 1966.

Gilson E., *History of Christian Philosophy in the Middle Ages*, trans. S. Zalewski, Warsaw 1987.

Hadot P., *What is Ancient Philosophy?*, trans. P. Domański, Warsaw 2000.

Irwin T., *The Development of Ethics. A Historical and Critical Study*, Oxford 2007.

Jaeger W., *Paideia*, trans. M. Plezia, Warsaw 1962–1964.

Krokiewicz A., *Outline of Greek Philosophy*, Warsaw 1997.

Laertius D., *Lives and Views of Famous Philosophers*, trans. I. Krońska, K. Leśniak, W. Olszewski, Warsaw 1984.

Legowicz J. (ed.), *Ancient Philosophy of Greece and Rome. Selected Texts from the History of Philosophy*, PWN, Warsaw 1968.

MacIntyre A., *A Brief History of Ethics*, trans. A. Chmielewski, Warsaw 1995.

MacIntyre A., *Heritage of Virtue*, trans. A. Chmielewski, Warsaw 1996.

Maritain J., *Moral Philosophy. An Historical and Critical Survey of the Great Systems*, New York 1964.

Mullach F.W.A., *Fragmenta Philosophorum Graecorum*, vol. I, Paris 1883.

Reale G., *History of Ancient Philosophy*, trans. M. Podbielski, Lublin 1993.

Rowe Ch., *Ethics of ancient Greece*, [in:] P. Singer, *A Companion to Ethics*, Basil Blackwell, New York, 1991, pp. 159–160.

Szlezak T.A., *Platon und die Scheiftlichkeit der Philosophie*, New York 1985.

Szlezak T.A., *Die Idee des Guten in Platons Politeia*, Sankt Augustin 2003.

Tatarkiewicz W., *History of Philosophy*, vol. I, Warsaw 1958.

Usener H., *Epicurea*, Leipzig 1887.

Vander Waerdt P.A. (ed.), *The Socratic Movement*, Ithaca 1994.

Vlasos G., *Socratic Studies*, Cambridge University Press 1995.

Voegelin E., *History of Political Ideas*, University of Missouri Press, 1997.

Annex

Figures

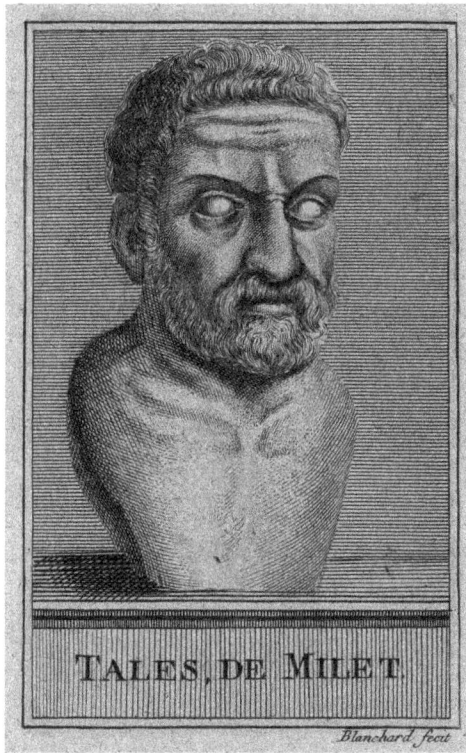

Thales of Miletus. Source: https://commons.wikimedia.org/wiki/File:Thales_of_
Miletus._Line_engraving_by_Blanchard._Wellcome_V0005771.jpg. Original
description: "V0005771 Thales of Miletus. Line engraving by Blanchard."
Credit: Wellcome Library, London. Wellcome Images images@wellcome.ac.uk
http://wellcomeimages.org. Image licensed under CC BY 4.0 license.

Pythagoras of Samos. Source: https://commons.wikimedia.org/wiki/
File:Kapitolinischer_Pythagoras.jpg. Photographer: Galilea/de.wikipedia.org.
Original description: "Busto di Pitagora. Copia romana di originale greco. Musei
Capitolini, Roma." Image licensed under CC-BY-SA 3.0 license.

Democritus of Abdera. Source: https://commons.wikimedia.org/wiki/
File:Filosofo_detto_democrito,_da_villa_dei_papiri,_peristilio_quadrato.JPG.
Photographer: Sailko/commons.wikimedia.org. Original description: "Ancient
Roman art from the Villa of the Papyri (Herculaneum)." Image licensed under
CC-BY-3.0 license.

Heraclitus of Ephesus. Source: https://commons.wikimedia.org/wiki/
File:Heraclitus_of_Ephesius,_Ionian_philosopher,_at_Ephesus._Wellcome_
L0002557.jpg. Photographer: J. Faber. Title: "Heraclitus of Ephesius, Ionian
philosopher, at Ephesus." Credit: Wellcome Library, London. Wellcome
Images: images@wellcome.ac.uk, http://wellcomeimages.org. Image licensed
under CC-BY-4.0 license.

Socrates. Source: https://commons.wikimedia.org/wiki/File:Socrates_Louvre.jpg. Photographer: Eric Gaba (Wikimedia Commons user: Sting). Original description: "Portrait of Socrates. Marble, Roman artwork (1st century), perhaps a copy of a lost bronze statue made by Lysippos." Image licensed under CC-BY-SA-2.5 license.

Platon. Source: https://commons.wikimedia.org/wiki/File:Head_Platon,_Glyptothek_Munich_548_120363.jpg. Photographer: Zde/commons.wikimedia.org. Original description: "Plato's head. Roman work after Greek sculpture from Silanion, around 347 BC. Glyptothek Munich Inv. N. 548." Image licensed under CC-BY-SA-3.0 license.

Aristotle. Source: https://de.wikipedia.org/wiki/Datei:Aristotle_Altemps_Inv8575.jpg. Photographer: Wikimedia Commons user: Jastrow. Image in the public domain.

Aristippus of Cyrene. Source: https://commons.wikimedia.org/wiki/
File:Aristippus_in_Thomas_Stanley_History_of_Philosophy.jpg. Original
source: Thomas Stanley, 1655, "The history of philosophy: containing the lives,
opinions, actions and Discourses of the Philosophers of every Sect, illustrated
with effigies of divers of them." Author unknown. Image in the public domain
(CC-PD-Art).

Epicurus of Samos Source: https://commons.wikimedia.org/wiki/File:Epikouros_Met_11.90.jpg. Photographer: Marie-Lan Nguyen. Original description: "Head of Epikouros. Roman copy of the Imperial era (AD 2nd century) after a Greek original of the 1st half of the 3rd century BC." Image licensed under CC BY-SA 2.0 license.

Antisthenes. Source: https://commons.wikimedia.org/wiki/File:Bust_of_
Antisthenes_(2459020131).jpg. Photographer: allen watkin/Flickr. Original
description: "Antisthenes, founder of the Cynic school. Marble, Roman copy
after a lost Hellenistic original." Image licensed under CC-BY-SA-2.0.

DIOGENES

Apud F. Ursinus in marmore.

Diogenes of Sinope. Source: https://commons.wikimedia.org/wiki/File:Diogenes_of_Sinope.jpg. Image in the public domain (CC-PD-Old).

Zeno of Citium. Source: https://commons.wikimedia.org/wiki/File:Zeno_of_
Citium_pushkin.jpg. Original description: "Herma of Zeno of Citium. Cast in
Pushkin museum from original in Naples." Photographer: Wikimedia Commons
user: shakko. Image licensed under CC-BY-SA-3.0 license.

PYRRHO.

Pyrrho of Elis. Source: https://commons.wikimedia.org/wiki/File:Pyrrho_in_
Thomas_Stanley_History_of_Philosophy.jpg. Author unknown. Image in the
public domain (CC-PD-1923).

Philo of Alexandria. Source: https://commons.wikimedia.org/wiki/
File:PhiloThevet.jpg. Author: André Thévet. Image in the public domain
(CC-PD-1923).

Plotinus. Source: https://commons.wikimedia.org/wiki/File:Testa_di_plotino,_
III_secolo,_dalla_domus_del_filosofo.JPG. Photographer: Wikimedia Commons
user: Sailko. Original description: "Ancient Roman busts in the Museo Ostiense
(Ostia Antica)." Image licensed under CC-BY-3.0 license.

Lucius Annaeus Seneca. Source: https://commons.wikimedia.org/wiki/File:0_
Portrait_de_S%C3%A9n%C3%A8que_d%27apr%C3%A8s_l%27antique_-_
Lucas_Vorsterman.JPG. This illustration was made by: Jean-Pol GRANDMONT.
Image in the public domain (CC-PD-Art-old-100).

Marcus Aurelius. Source: https://commons.wikimedia.org/wiki/File:Marcus_
Aurelius_Metropolitan_Museum.png. Photographer: Wikimedia Commons
user: Steerpike. Original description: "Marble portrait bust of Marcus Aurelius.
Roman, Antonine period, 161–180 AD. Metropolitan Museum of Art,
New York."

Cicero. Source: https://commons.wikimedia.org/wiki/File:Marcus_Tullius_ Cicero_(_106_-_43_v._Chr)_---_Colonia_Ulpia_Traiana,_Xanten_Niederrhein_ (7716385800).jpg. Photographer: Heribert Pohl. Image licensed under CC-BY-SA-2.0 license.

Titus Lucretius Carus. Source: https://commons.wikimedia.org/wiki/
File:Lucretius_Rome.jpg. Photographer: Wikimedia Commons user: StefanoRR.
Author: Unknown Italian artist. Image in the public domain (PD-anon-1923).

Quintus Septimius Tertulianus. Source: https://commons.wikimedia.org/wiki/
File:Quintus_Septimius_Florens_Tertullianus.gif. Author: unknown. Image in the
public domain (CC-PD-Art-old).

Augustine of Hippo. Source: https://commons.wikimedia.org/wiki/File:Augustine_of_Hippo.jpg. Original source: "Hundred Greatest Men," The. New York: D. Appleton & Company, 1885. Image in the public domain (CC-PD-old).

Philosophy and Cultural Studies Revisited /
Historisch-genetische Studien zur Philosophie und Kulturgeschichte

Editd by/herausgegeben von Seweryn Blandzi

Band 1 Dorota Muszytowska / Janusz Kręcidło / Anna Szczepan-Wojnarska (eds.): Jerusalem as the Text of Culture. 2018.

Band 2 Dorota Probucka (ed.): Contemporary Moral Dilemmas. 2018.

Band 3 Ján Zozuľak: Inquiries into Byzantine Philosophy. 2018.

Band 4 Marek Piechowiak: Plato's Conception of Justice and the Question of Human Dignity. 2018.

Band 5 Dorota Probucka: Ethics in Ancient Greece and Rome. 2019.

www.peterlang.com